Recruiting and Retaining Teachers

Understanding why teachers
teach

Anne D. Cockburn &
Terry Haydn

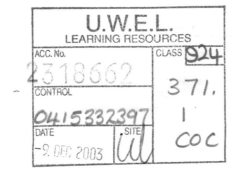

 RoutledgeFalmer
Taylor & Francis Group

LONDON AND NEW YORK

First published 2004 by RoutledgeFalmer
11 New Fetter Lane, London EC4P 4EE

Simultaneously published in the USA and Canada
by RoutledgeFalmer
29 West 35th Street, New York, NY 10001

RoutledgeFalmer is an imprint of the Taylor & Francis Group

© 2004 Anne D. Cockburn & Terry Haydn

Typeset in Goudy by Keystroke, Jacaranda Lodge, Wolverhampton
Printed and bound in Great Britain by Biddles Ltd, King's Lynn

British Library Cataloguing in Publication Data
A catalogue record for this book is available from the British Library

Library of Congress Cataloging-in-Publication Data
Cockburn, Anne.
    Recruiting and retaining teachers : understanding why teachers
teach/
Anne D. Cockburn & Terry Haydn.
        p. cm.
    Includes bibliographical references and index.
    ISBN 0–415–33239–7 (hard alk. paper) —
    ISBN 0–415–28439–2 (pbk. : alk. paper)
    1. Teachers—Recruiting—Great Britain. 2. Teachers—Selection
and appointment—Great Britain. 3. Teachers—Job satisfaction—
Great Britain. I. Haydn, Terry, 1951– II. Title.
    LB2835.28.G7C63 2004
    331.7′6113711′00941—dc21   2003013494

Contents

List of Figures

List of Tables

Introduction and acknowledgements

This book was written at a time of teacher shortage in the UK but goes far beyond that. It was specifically written for LEA and government policy makers and headteachers but it is intended for a far broader readership. We are confident in writing such sentences, for our researches into teacher supply demonstrate that it is an issue which touches many aspects of school and, indeed, community life. On examining how the crises in the teacher supply and demand balance arose, it is clear that the problem is multifaceted and, although effective strategies are available for addressing the problem, they frequently have not been applied. This, in our view, is not because they are expensive and complex. Rather, we argue, there has been insufficient understanding of teachers as people – with lives, aspirations and an abundance of fine qualities – and the situations in which they work. Neither, we suggest, has there been sufficient insight into what individuals seek in their working lives and the potential of teaching as a profession. We do not claim to have all the answers but, in writing this book, we discovered much and, on reading it, we hope that you will develop a broader understanding of teaching, schools and the teaching profession.

The negative aspects of being a teacher in the UK at the present time have been widely explored and documented over the past few years (see Chapter 1) but the factors that persuade many people to go into teaching and stay teaching in the face of these deterrents has been less extensively researched. Listening to the voices of teachers and trainee teachers is one way of gaining a better understanding about what helps them enjoy their work. Finding out what young people at universities and in sixth forms *who are considering teaching as a career* hope to get out of life in teaching is another way of providing better intelligence for those who shape the quality of teachers' working lives.

As well as drawing on recent research studies on teacher recruitment and retention, our work is based on a national survey of over 2,000 sixth formers and third-year undergraduates, on surveys of our own primary and secondary trainees and on over 80 interviews with teachers, from headteachers to NQTs.

We owe thanks to many people in the production of this book. In particular we would like to thank the CfBT and Town Close Charity for their financial support for studies undertaken. We very gratefully acknowledge the work of our colleague Ann Oliver who has been a co-researcher on several of our projects. Anna Clarkson and her colleagues also merit much thanks for being unfailingly patient and understanding about the time it has taken us to produce this book. We also greatly appreciate the help of students and sixth formers for finding time to complete questionnaires and being interviewed. We are grateful to headteacher Paul Grant for allowing access to the school, pupils and teachers at Robert Clack School, Dagenham, and for giving permission for the school to be identified in this book. Thanks also to Helen Harding for deciphering Anne's scrawl and unravelling the logic of her many inserts and crossings out. Finally, thanks to the many teachers who gave their time to tell us of the trials and tribulations of their lives and work. We have great admiration for teachers and it is to them we dedicate this book.

Anne Cockburn and Terry Haydn
University of East Anglia
May 2003

Chapter 1

Recruiting and retaining good teachers: a non-trivial facet of education policy

> A profound sentiment of the importance of his work must sustain and animate the teacher; the austere pleasure of having served mankind and contributed to the public weal must be worthy payment which his conscience alone gives him. It is his glory to use himself up in sacrifices and to expect his reward only from God.
>
> (F. Guizot, 1833, explaining to French
> teachers why their pay was so low)[1]

'Teachers make a difference'

One of the few uncontested areas of education policy is the importance of attracting and retaining well motivated, able and intelligent graduates into teaching. The importance of teacher recruitment and retention is acknowledged in the statements and actions of politicians and policy makers in this area. In a speech to the Labour Party Conference, the then secretary of state for education, David Blunkett, described teachers as 'our most precious asset' (*Guardian*, 2 October 2000), and the prime minister, Tony Blair, pledged to make teaching 'the most prestigious profession in the country attracting the brightest and best trainees', stating that 'there is no more important job in the country today' (speech to London headteachers, 23 November 2000).

The Teacher Training Agency has expressed the hope that teaching will become one of the three most sought after professions, and that competition for places in Initial Teacher Training (ITT) will be sufficiently fierce that all successful applicants will have either first class or upper second class degrees. Concern over both the supply of teachers and the quality of those entering the profession was acknowledged in the government's Green Paper, *Teachers: Meeting the Challenge of Change*

(DfEE 1998), with its stated objective 'to recruit, retain and motivate high quality teachers', and create a 'world class' teaching force, and, more recently, the establishment of a special unit to tackle the problem of teacher recruitment (*Times Educational Supplement*, 8 December 2000).

What we have written in this book draws in part on our own research and on a large number of other recent studies in this field. It draws on the public debate on teacher recruitment and retention which has been prominently featured in the national press as a result of the recent high profile of the problem of teacher supply and is influenced by our own experience of working in teacher education over a number of years. A significant proportion of our time is spent visiting students in schools, talking to teachers and headteachers and interviewing prospective applicants for our PGCE Partnership Course. It is not possible to do this work without becoming aware of the importance of getting the right human 'raw materials' into teacher education, and into schools, in the first place.

Although good training and induction, and inspirational mentoring can make a substantial difference to the speed at which trainee teachers develop, and the extent to which they will move towards excellence, we have never encountered any university tutor, mentor or headteacher who believes that it is possible to make a good teacher out of just about any graduate who tumbles out of university.

The range of skills, attributes and personal qualities required to be a good teacher is much broader than that required to be successful in securing an undergraduate degree. The failure of John Patten's 'Mums Army' scheme and the more recent controversies over the deployment of teaching assistants are indications of the acceptance by parents, governors, teachers and headteachers that whatever the quality of support staff, the ICT facilities, or the 'rollout' of government teaching and learning strategies, the principal determinant of the quality of education which pupils will receive is the quality and calibre of the classroom teacher. This consensus is reinforced by the fact that unlike perceptions of other professions, adult views about teachers are informed by first-hand experience. At least three newspapers run a weekly column on 'My best teacher'; we are not aware of the existence of 'My best bank manager' or 'My best accountant' equivalents.

The importance of understanding why *studying job satisfaction* teachers teach and what they want to get out of the job

In 1997, one of the government's responses to the haemorrhaging of experienced teachers from the profession was to make it more difficult for them to take early retirement. There is little evidence to suggest that much thought was given to exploring *why* increasingly large numbers of teachers wanted to get out of teaching, or to the wisdom of making those who wanted to leave the profession continue until retirement age.

Since then, the government has spent millions of pounds on the problem of teacher recruitment and retention, and launched a range of policy initiatives to try to increase the number of people going into teaching. This has included the payment of a 'training salary' of £6,000 to those embarking on PGCE courses (£10,000 in shortage subjects), the promotion of alternative routes into teaching, the restructuring of the profession in terms of 'threshold' pay and performance management, the funding of a range of initiatives to encourage 'returners', and high profile advertising campaigns and glossy magazines to persuade people into a career in teaching. Many of these initiatives emanated from the Cabinet Office, the product of people who did not themselves have a background in teaching. This is not to suggest that the initiatives are other than well intended, but that people who go into journalism, politics and administration are likely to have a different 'mind-set' to people who go into teaching and to have a limited understanding of why teachers teach and what are the principal attractions and deterrents of the job. Kyriacou and Coulthard's study of undergraduates' perceptions of teaching as a career found that those who were still considering teaching as a possible career placed 'Fast Track' schemes and 'salaries based on performance' at the bottom of their list of factors which might encourage them to enter the profession. They suggest that advertising campaigns to attract young people into the teaching profession have been flawed in their focus (Kyriacou and Coulthard 2000) and have not taken sufficient account of what is known about the views of young people who are 'biddable' to the idea of going into teaching. As House (2000: 14) argues,

[margin note: money for recruiting teachers]

> government leaders . . . are mistaken in their initiatives because they are too far removed from educational work, too wedded to powerful interests, too imbued with misleading ideologies and simply misinformed. Thus, educational policies dissolve into ineffectiveness, to be replaced by other mistaken and ineffective policies.

Some of the initiatives were introduced in spite the fact that opinion polls suggested that a substantial majority of teachers (in some cases over 90 per cent) did not think that they were a good idea. The idea that 'Fast Track' routes would attract large numbers of high-calibre graduates into the profession has not yet proved successful, and Howson (2002a) describes the distribution of modular and part-time teacher training courses as 'at best haphazard, and at worst, downright random'. As Ted Wragg has pointed out (*TES*, 7 February 2003), headteachers were not canvassed to sound out the feasibility and good sense of the initiatives. There was, until recently, little to suggest that policies to improve teacher recruitment and retention took into account the increasing body of research evidence on the factors which were deterring people from entering and remaining in teaching.

One of the principal propositions of this book is that politicians, policy makers and schools need to acquire and develop 'good intelligence' on what attracts, motivates and fulfils teachers, what stops them enjoying their work, what is most important to them and what is 'negotiable'. Headteachers and senior managers, as teachers themselves and as people who spend their working lives in close contact with teachers, have a much more grounded understanding of what teachers want and need. There is, nonetheless, a need for them to have as full and up-to-date an understanding as possible about what factors incline teachers to move on to other schools and what factors are most influential to trainees choosing their first post.

A survey of the research findings in the area of career choice over the past decade reveals that although financial remuneration and promotion prospects play a part in young people's career aspirations, they are only two factors amongst many which influence career choice (Arnold *et al.* 1991; Csikszentmihalyi 1992; Cockburn *et al.* 2000; Doyle 2000). There are several areas of employment which offer neither high levels of remuneration nor secure pathways to promotion (for instance journalism, museums officers) which consistently attract large numbers of entrants.

Teachers have never been highly paid. If people wanted to make lots of money and then retire early, buy a yacht and a home abroad, they would not contemplate going into teaching. Even within the public sector, their remuneration has tended to be less generous than that of other groups. It is not just in England that the salaries paid to teachers have lagged behind those of doctors and lawyers. Neither does teaching generally offer the prospect of a luxuriously attractive working environment. Teachers often never get their own personal office space in the way that is still reasonably common in, for instance, higher education. Schools are not usually areas of outstanding architectural merit. Most of them are fairly old, down at heel and, at best, utilitarian in their setting. Nor is teaching (rightly or wrongly) considered a prestigious or glamorous job. It does not have the cachet or appeal of a career in politics or journalism. Unfortunately, there are many people who do not even think that teaching is a difficult and challenging job; as one university reference we received commented, 'While she is not a high flier, I imagine that she would not find a PGCE course over demanding.' In spite of this, there are many people who still choose to go into teaching.

One of the first steps in addressing the problem of teacher recruitment and retention, for policy makers and for schools, is to understand what it is about teaching that makes people want to do it in spite of the limited potential it offers for personal affluence, pleasant working conditions and social kudos. Several research studies have shown that the sort of challenges that teaching offers appeal to a particular sub-set of the school and undergraduate populations (see, for example, Kyriacou and Coulthard 2000; Cockburn et al. 2001; McKernan and Taylor 2002). By the sixth form, and as undergraduates, many people have already made up their mind that teaching is definitely not for them. Kyriacou's survey of undergraduates showed of a sample of 298 undergraduates, 102 had definitely discounted the option of teaching, 40 were 'seriously considering' it and 155 were 'undecided'. Our own survey of over 2,000 young people (1,675 sixth formers and 346 third-year undergraduates) showed that amongst school leavers, although only 7.3 per cent of respondents felt that they probably or definitely would go into teaching, a further 17.4 per cent were still considering teaching as a possible career. Whereas under 10 per cent of third-year undergraduates expressed a firm commitment to enter teaching, a further 20 per cent were still considering it as a possibility.

These figures demonstrate that there is 'a lot to play for', in that if politicians, policy makers and schools respond constructively to the 'intelligence' about what young people predisposed to teaching are looking for in a career, it could make a massive difference to the number of high-quality entrants to the profession.

Not a short-term problem?

The provision and retention of a high-calibre, highly motivated teaching force is not a new problem, or one which is limited to the United Kingdom. Posner and Tikly (2002: 211) argue that the mathematical education of a majority of the population of England and Wales has been hampered by a shortfall in the quality and quantity of mathematics teachers 'for over a century'. The myth that teacher supply is only a problem in times of economic upturn and that recession will redress any deficiencies in supply has been eroded by the duration of teacher shortages, the emergence of 'structural' problems (such as the reluctance of young people to undertake degree courses in particular National Curriculum subjects such as maths and science) and the fact that in some parts of the country, teachers' salaries do not offer a realistic possibility of them owning their own homes. Although, demographically, the number of pupils entering primary schools is plateauing, we are still several years away from a situation where there will be an overall decrease in pupil numbers. Howson (2002a) stresses both the urgency and the long-term nature of the problem of teacher supply:

> The need to introduce some coherence into teacher supply is becoming urgent. Over the next decade, record numbers of teachers will retire. Even if retention rates amongst younger teachers are improved, workload and changing learning styles will almost certainly mean an increase in the number of graduates needed for teaching and other associated posts in schools.
>
> Time is running out. Assuming the next general election is in the autumn of 2005 or early 2006, to meet its election pledge of 10,000 extra teachers by the end of this parliament the government will need to increase overall teacher numbers by about 2,500 a year. After the comprehensive spending review, the money is there – but will there be the people?[2]

Even this stern warning of the scale of the problem focuses principally on the number of teachers, rather than issues of quality. In the same article, Howson also raises concerns about teacher quality, pointing to the rapid increase in the number of untrained instructors who can now be referred to as 'teachers' by the DfES.

There is also evidence to suggest that the challenge of persuading substantial numbers of the most able and well qualified young people to enter the teaching profession is proving increasingly difficult, worldwide. In 1998, Jerome T. Murphy, dean of the Harvard Graduate School of Education, warned that 'too many talented students are not entering the teaching profession because of better opportunities elsewhere' (*Boston Globe*, 25 July), and these concerns have been echoed more recently by the director of a major teacher recruitment agency, whose network covers four continents, who refers to:

A worldwide problem where 13 out of 15 European Union States face teacher shortages and the USA is in the grip of the biggest recruitment crisis for a generation. Several Australian states are experiencing difficulties. New Zealand is marketing its vacancies throughout the European World, and even Canada, which has some of the highest paid teachers on the planet, cannot always fill its maths and science posts.

(King 2000)

Howson (1999) claims that 'only Portugal and Austria appear to have even half the required number of under-30s in teaching', and a recent European conference on teacher supply noted Rotterdam, New York, Berlin and London as particular problem areas in terms of both the recruitment and the retention of teachers (*TES*, 8 December 2000).

The global nature of the problem of teacher supply adds a further dimension to concerns about the creation and maintenance of a high-calibre, highly motivated teaching force. The UK has in recent years been a net importer of teachers, but Howson (1999) speculates that 'the competition for teachers is likely to become global during the next decade', with countries offering a range of incentives to attract well-qualified teachers. Research by Ingersoll (2001) and Bracey (2002) suggests that the American experience of teacher supply closely mirrors our own, with 'out of field' teaching increasing to over 24 per cent and almost half of new recruits to the profession leaving within five years. British newspapers have already started to feature advertisements for teachers to work in the United States, and net 'exporters' of teachers are expressing concern about the burden of training teachers who are going to work elsewhere ('Schools robbing third world of trained teachers', *Guardian*, 29 March 2002). Our survey of our own trainees' intentions for their future career development suggests that the possibility of teaching abroad is an attraction for substantial numbers of them (see Chapter 3). Britain is not the only country that will have to give careful thought to the quality of teachers' working lives and to the question of how to attract teachers from other countries to compensate for a shortfall of 'home grown' teachers.

All this suggests that teacher supply will be, at least, a medium-term problem and that for the foreseeable future, heads, senior management teams and governors will need to give considerable thought to how their schools are going to attract and retain good teachers.

In another sense, the issues of teacher recruitment and retention are always going to be a key concern of schools. One of the key issues to emerge from recent problems in these areas is the difference between filling teacher vacancies with 'a body' to put in front of a class and getting hold of the best, brightest and most committed teachers emerging from their training. Current Ofsted methodology for the inspection of initial teacher training (ITT) requires teacher trainers to rank all trainees from grade 1 to 4. Grade 1 equates to 'Very good in all areas, with some outstanding features'; these student teachers are often dauntingly good, even within the course of their professional training, and are likely to be very effective teachers, even in their NQT year. Grade 2 equals 'Good in all areas with no significant weaknesses', Grade 3 signifies that they are 'adequate', and Grade 4, unsatisfactory (and therefore not eligible to be awarded Qualified Teacher Status (QTS)). Even in our partnership, where we have high numbers of applications for the course in nearly all subjects, and can therefore afford to be very selective about which applicants to take on, not all trainees will be 'Very good across all areas with several outstanding features' *within the course of the PGCE year*. (A great number of those who do not reach Grade 1 quickly develop into excellent teachers after they have left the course.)

Given current shortages in many school subjects, outstanding trainees are aware that they are in a 'sellers' market' and that they can, in effect, choose from a large number of schools that would be keen to employ them. (The desperate position in some subjects means that there have been occasions where trainees have been offered teaching posts before the start of their school placements). Although starting salary and other induce- ments such as the provision of a laptop computer and payment of salary from June rather than September are not inconsequential considerations in their decision, the survey of our trainees as to which factors influenced their choice of first appointment revealed that their perception of how happy they would be in their work was generally a more important consideration (see Chapter 3).

Given the finite number of 'first-class' trainees, schools are increasingly having to give time and thought to how to ensure that they can maximise their attractiveness to new entrants to the profession, particularly in shortage subject areas, in the same way that companies court 'the cream' of the undergraduate population in an attempt to secure as many 'high- fliers' as possible. Our experience suggests that some schools have moved much more radically than others in this area (see Chapter 6).

The scale of the problem of teacher supply: looking beyond vacancy rates

There has been a tendency for government agencies to underplay the scale of the problem of teacher supply by claiming that teacher shortages are only a problem in some parts of the country, pointing out that the 'scare stories' of a widespread four-day teaching week because of teacher shortages have not been realised,[3] and pointing to fairly unsensational teacher vacancy rates. In its 1999 submission to the School Teachers' Review body, the DfEE steadfastly refused to accept that there was a significant problem with teacher supply, stating that 'despite suggestions to the contrary in the media, figures on teacher vacancies suggest that there is no substantial shortage of teachers across England and Wales as a whole' (DfEE 1999).

Although the Chief Inspector for Schools appeared to confirm the DfEE line in 2002, stating that 'teacher supply is not in dire or desperate straits across the piste' (*TES*, 3 May 2002), a subsequent Ofsted report on recruitment and retention reiterated Mike Tomlinson's earlier concern (*TES*, 7 December 2001) that 'serious recruitment difficulties' were making it much more difficult for headteachers to ensure good teaching and high standards.

> Difficulties in recruiting and retaining teachers are increasing. Few of the LEAs have clear policies for assuring the supply and quality of teachers. The need to resort to a series of temporary or acting arrangements is proving disruptive for schools and for children's education.
>
> (Ofsted 2002)

The DfES has tended to use the vacancy rate statistics and overall increases in the number of teachers employed to refute suggestions that there is in any sense a 'crisis' in teacher supply. DfEE estimates of vacancy rates in 2001 were 0.5 per cent of the teaching force for primary and 0.8 per cent for secondary (DfEE 2001). Statistics for 2002 suggested an overall vacancy rate of 1.2 per cent and an increase of 9,400 in the number of teachers in full-time posts, leading schools minister David Miliband to argue that teacher supply was only a problem in some areas and that 'the statistics spoke for themselves' (*TES*, 9 August 2002).

However, as Howson (*TES*, 14 February 2003) points out, 'If a school has a vacancy it cannot fill, it has three options: it can continue to show the vacancy, suppress it by reducing the timetable or avoid it by recruiting outside the required specialism and using non-specialists to teach the shortage subject.' Our experience within our own PGCE partnership suggests that the third option is now common practice.

At a time when 'official' sources were playing down any suggestion of a 'crisis' in teacher supply, Ian Pitman, chair of Timeplan Supply Agency, described the situation in England as 'unbelievable . . . the shortage has been absolutely desperate' (*TES*, 18 August 2000).

The use of vacancy rates and total teacher numbers as the principal indicators of teacher supply and the tendency for government ministers and DfES officials to take a bullish line on the question of teacher shortages has evinced a counter-reaction from heads and senior managers in schools who feel that teacher shortages are not being taken sufficiently seriously. The TES has regularly featured articles on the difficulties which schools are facing in recruiting and retaining good teachers. Smithers and Robinson (2000) go as far as to describe the January 'snapshot' of teacher vacancies as misleading. There are several good reasons to look beyond the issue of vacancy rates in considering the issue of teacher supply.

As Menter (2002) points out, the system of allocating training places to providers based on the quality of provision, as reflected by Ofsted inspection grades, is insensitive to regional demand for teachers. Given the strong tendency for teachers to seek employment close to the location of their initial training (Ross 2001), the total number of teachers being produced nationally is not necessarily in the right places to respond to regional needs. The assumption that those who cannot find a post in the area they prefer will naturally gravitate to vacancies elsewhere rather than do something else may be misplaced. Nor are regional dimensions to teacher supply influenced solely by house prices, in spite of the particularly acute shortages in much of London (Hutchings *et al.* 2000). Although in terms of recent media coverage this has been perhaps the most high-profile factor, the survey of our trainees in East Anglia showed that a proportion of them were reluctant to take up posts 'out in the sticks' and were looking to return to London, the south-east, or to big cities in spite of the implications for housing costs (see Chapter 3). Nor is it possible to conclude that teacher supply is only a problem in challenging inner-city schools. Recent press reports note serious problems in teacher supply at schools such as Cheltenham Ladies College and Lady Margaret School London, schools riding high in the GCSE and A-level league tables. In asking a number of secondary headteachers in the eastern region whether or not their school had difficulties in securing a satisfactory cohort of teachers across all subjects, we were unable to find any who said that this was 'not a problem'. The increasingly desperate measures which some schools are resorting to in order to fill vacancies give some indication that teacher supply is not unproblematic. Examples include offering overseas teachers employment without face-to-face or telephone interview, offering young teachers a year's accommodation in the YMCA (TES, 26 April 2002), sending pupils to stand in supermarkets with badges saying 'Teach me please' (Guardian, 17 May 2001) and offering new staff the use of the headteacher's Mercedes at weekends (TES, 12 April 2002).

Another of the consequences of recent shortages has been that heads and senior managers are having to spend increasing amounts of their time attending to staffing issues. In discussions with headteachers, several spoke of their frustration at the extremely time-consuming and inefficient activities they had to become embroiled in when attempting to fill posts in shortage subjects, in addition to the costs of readvertising posts and having to replace teachers from abroad who sometimes failed to 'stay the course' of the school year. Other 'collateral' implications of difficulties in recruiting a full and stable cohort of staff and having a secure system for providing supply cover include not being able to release staff to go on training courses – at some cost to staff morale – and the 'vicious circle' of not being able to offer placements to teacher trainees because of instability and high turnover in departments. In schools which are really struggling to put bodies in front of classes, there is also the temptation to push trainees into whole class teaching too quickly, or to use them to substitute for absent colleagues just to 'plug the gaps' in what is sometimes a desperate attempt to avoid having to send pupils home, or having them supervised in the school hall in large groups.

Even more seriously, the reliance on citing vacancy rates to rebut suggestions of problems with teacher supply disguises real concerns over teacher subject specialisms. One of the concerns is, in Howson's words, 'Who is teaching what subjects, and to whom in our schools?' (Howson 2002a). Although the government has not recently published any figures on the extent to which teachers are teaching 'out of field', and so it is difficult to quantify the extent of this practice, it is generally accepted that getting staff to teach subjects for which they have not been professionally trained is one of the ways in which schools cope with teacher shortages in particular subjects. A TES/SHA survey estimated that more than 3,200 teachers are taking maths, English, science and languages lessons for which they have no professional training (TES, 30 August 2002), and Christine Whatford, director of education in Hammersmith and Fulham, recently suggested that most teachers of maths in the capital were not qualified in the subject (*TES*, 14 February 2003). More than one senior member of staff that we spoke to described advertising for a maths teacher as 'a joke', and several schools were clearly going to extraordinary lengths to get some sort of 'maths' teacher in front of classes.

The *TES/SHA* survey suggests that another consequence of high turnover and instability in shortage subject departments is the difficulty of finding someone to step in as head of department in a situation where there are several poorly qualified, inexperienced or makeshift teachers. In the words of John Dunford, general secretary of SHA,

> The adverse effects of teacher shortage tend to fall disproportionately on heads of department. Being head of a maths department in which there are no other qualified teachers and a couple of temporary appointments is a very difficult job. People are just not willing to take it on.
>
> (quoted in *TES*, 30 August 2002)

The study of teacher supply and retention in six London boroughs (Hutchings *et al.* 2000) suggests that this problem may extend all the way up to headship appointments, with only 61 per cent of advertisements resulting in appointments, an average of only 4.2 applications per post, and 25 per cent of cases where it was not possible to shortlist (see also Groves 2001).

For all the gravity of these 'collateral' effects of problems in teacher supply, the most serious concern remains that of teacher quality. Do current difficulties in teacher supply mean that, in desperation, some teachers are being offered posts who are not 'up to it' and who would not 'in better times' gain permanent posts? As early as 1974, OECD research on teacher supply moved beyond an emphasis on teacher numbers towards an analysis of factors impacting on teacher quality (OECD 1974). Recent DfES and ministerial rebuttals of the idea that there are teacher shortages have tended to focus on numbers rather than quality issues.

Several of the heads we spoke to suggested that although fields were generally smaller and often 'shortlisting' for interview was no longer necessary, there was still a large majority of cases where perfectly satisfactory appointments could be made, and that short-term expedients, such as recruiting through agencies and 'shuffling', arrangements could often get schools through temporary difficulties where this was not the case, even if arrangements and circumstances were less than ideal. The 2002 *TES/SHA* survey of 828 state and private secondary schools indicated, however, that many heads were unhappy with the quality of many of the appointments they had made, with nearly a fifth of teachers appointed in the term of the survey adjudged to be unsatisfactory, and acknowledging that sometimes they were having to settle for people who were not 'up to the job'. One head admitted that he was appointing 'people you would not have previously have looked at' (*TES*, 30 August 2002). Given the general acknowledgement of the scale of damage that can be done by poor and unsatisfactory teachers, this is perhaps the most worrying aspect of the problem of teacher supply.

The changing nature of the problem

Even within the last three years, the nature of the problem of teacher supply has changed significantly. A review of research on teacher supply in the UK by the National Foundation for Educational Research (NFER) (2000: 6) concluded that:

> The recruitment of students to initial teacher-training courses has been in decline over most of the last decade, a problem which has been particularly acute at the secondary level. Difficulties have also been encountered in retaining teachers in the profession. Both newly qualified and experienced teachers have left the profession for a variety of reasons, such as stress, low morale and job dissatisfaction. Senior managers have sought early retirement. These difficulties in recruiting trainees and retaining teachers have led to teacher shortages in both primary and secondary schools.

Since the NFER survey, the *nature* of the problem has changed. After several years of disappointing recruitment to ITT courses, the overall pattern of recruitment to ITT courses has been much healthier, with a remarkable upturn in the number of people applying to go into teaching – up by almost two-thirds since the introduction of training bursaries, with 16,600 secondary applications in England and Wales by March 2003, as against around 10,000 in March 2000 (*TES*, 4 April 2003).

In spite of these generally encouraging increases, there is still a structural problem in terms of the number of people going into university to study for science and maths degrees, and there are still PGCE courses which struggle to recruit to numbers in these and other subjects.

These increases have not been 'across the board', and big increases in 'problem' subjects such as maths (up by 84 per cent) physics, chemistry and ICT have not been so substantial that the problem of teacher supply in these areas has disappeared, while applications to teach Religious Education have declined, prompting recruitment expert John Howson (2003) to advocate that RE should join the list of subjects which attract the extra bonus of a £4,000 'Golden Hello'. Although maths and physics appear to be 'national' in terms of teacher shortages, there continue to be regional variations in terms which secondary subjects are most problematic. Howson (*TES*, 12 April 2003) notes shortages in music, modern foreign languages and chemistry as 'very worrying' areas, but several headteachers and LEA advisers we spoke to in the East of England now regarded English as one of the most challenging subjects in terms of teacher supply.

There have been different interpretations as to the reasons for this turnaround in the number of people choosing to embark on teacher training courses. In one speech Estelle Morris attributed the increase to the introduction of performance-related pay (together with the payment of training salaries to those entering initial training). The chief executive of the TTA, Ralph Tabberer, expressed his delight that more people were recognising 'the rewards and career opportunities that teaching offers' and attributed this to 'our successful marketing campaign "Those who can, teach", the government's new financial incentives, and greater efforts by training providers' (TTA Press Release 16/01, 1 November 2001).

Given that performance-related pay, training salaries and national advertising campaigns to attract people into teaching were introduced at roughly the same time, it is difficult to ascertain the precise 'weighting' that should be attached to these initiatives. Our own research (see Chapter 2) suggests that the initiative which seemed to have had a real impact on recruitment was the payment of training salaries to those entering PGCE, SCITT and GTP courses. (It is perhaps worth noting that these salaries have not been increased since their introduction).

Retention, retention, retention

Given the changing patterns of the past three years, the retention of teachers has emerged as a more important issue than simply getting people onto training courses to become teachers. This change was noted by Graham Lane, education spokesperson for the Association of Local Government, as early as 2000, when he suggested that 'the most serious problem is that 25–30 year olds are leaving the profession and not coming back' (quoted in *Observer*, 14 May 2000). In the Eastern region – an area with above average difficulties in terms of teacher supply

– one senior LEA official told us that 'if there wasn't a retention problem, there wouldn't be a recruitment problem'. This bears out Smithers and Robinson's claim (2000) that with adequate retention, the training targets set by the government would largely have solved the problems of teacher supply. The combination of trainees not completing their course, not choosing to go into teaching at the end of their course, or leaving the profession within three years amounts to a wastage rate estimated at between 40 and 52 per cent (Smithers and Robinson 2000; Howson 2002b). Again, there were significant regional variations, with London proving particularly problematic in terms of both recruitment and retention, and the eastern region and some parts of the north also encountering difficulties (Howson 1999, 2002a; DfEE 2000).

As Menter (2002: 2) notes, some senior policy makers have appeared to be surprisingly relaxed about the idea that people might be encouraged to think of teaching not as a career for life, but as an occupation that they might undertake for a few years before turning to another profession. Estelle Morris talked of teaching being 'increasingly one of those areas where people will move in and move out' (*Guardian*, 12 June 2002). This insouciance disregards the fact that there are more experienced professionals moving out of teaching than moving into it, and fewer trained teachers returning to the profession after a career break (Howson 2000; Penlington 2002). It also understates the value to schools of teachers who have *substantial* experience of teaching and working in schools and who have developed profound and extensive understanding of the many complex issues involved in teaching and learning, and of schools as organisations. Richard Ingersoll's research dispels the idea that one of the pivotal causes of inadequate school performance is the inability of schools to adequately staff classrooms with qualified teachers. Although his research was based on school staffing surveys, teacher exit interviews and teacher supply statistics in the United States, there are sufficient similarities to teacher 'turnover' in the UK to make his analysis pertinent to the situation in this country.

> The results of the analysis indicate that school staffing problems are not primarily due to teacher shortages, in the technical sense of an insufficient supply of qualified teachers. Rather the data indicate that school staffing problems are primarily due to excess demand resulting from a 'revolving door' – where large numbers of qualified teachers depart their jobs for reasons other than retirement. Moreover, the data show that the amount of turnover accounted for by retirement is relatively minor when compared to that associated

with other factors, such as teacher job dissatisfaction and teachers pursuing other jobs . . . Popular education initiatives such as teacher recruitment programmes will not solve the staffing problems of such schools if they do not also address the organisational sources of low teacher retention.

(Ingersoll, 2001: 499)

An interesting facet of our survey of young people's views on teachers and teaching was the extent to which 'social transmission' factors influenced their views. Several of those interviewed cited personal contacts and experience as being an influential part of their views about teachers and teaching. Some examples from the interview transcripts of third-year undergraduates are given below.

'**My boyfriend is a teacher** . . . I can see all the stress involved, I can see the amount of work involved, and outside of hours work. It doesn't stop when you get home, it just keeps on going.'

(RH, 29/3/00)

'I mean, **some of my friends actually are teachers**.'
(Cited pay and inspections as deterrents.) (W, 30/3/00)

'**Because my mum's a teacher,** and that's kind of like . . . that's kind of affected my whole view of teachers in general.'
(Cited long hours, administration and difficult pupils as deterrents.) (H, 4/4/00)

'**Both my parents are teachers** . . . I decided not to go into teaching basically, probably because of the bad press my parents gave it.'
(Cited lack of flexibility and autonomy as deterrents.)
(S, 28/11/99)

'**Well actually, I've got a friend who has tried** . . . He was voluntarily doing . . . joined a school on a Wednesday afternoon . . . He's totally put off by the fact of trying to keep children under control. And he sort of feels that you don't get paid enough for the stress he'd have to go under for doing that.'

'My perceptions of teachers personally changed because in the last few years **I've had several friends becoming teachers**.'
(Cited control, workload, National Curriculum and testing as deterrents.) (K, 4/1/00)

'I have five children myself and listening to teenagers talking about
what they get up to in school, I'm not sure I could handle it.'

(P, 11/11/99)

This suggests that Tabberer's earlier explanation for changing patterns in
teacher recruitment and retention – the impact of advertising campaigns,
government and TTA initiatives and incentives, and increased provider
proactivity – is at best a partial one. In the same way that everyone can
remember a good teacher, it would appear that most people know
someone who is a teacher or teacher trainee, whether as parent, partner,
friend or sibling, and that this personal contact has an influence on their
perceptions of teachers' work and teachers' lives.

The significance of social transmission factors is also noted by Pollard
(2001: 19):

> Quality is an issue and many inter-generational families of teachers
> no longer recommend the profession to their children. Although
> salaries have increased, very high proportions of qualified teachers
> of working age remain employed outside education and are reluctant
> to resume teaching. Access to early retirement has been made more
> difficult because of the scale of the professional outflow. Schools are
> severely pressured to find occasional staff for short-term cover.

Given this 'word of mouth' dimension to the views of young people
about what fulfils and what dismays teachers in their work, responding
appropriately and sensitively to our 'intelligence' about teachers' feelings
about their conditions of work and the quality of their working lives is
an important prerequisite to improving both teacher supply and teacher
retention. In the words of Ted Wragg (2000) 'Making the current generation of teachers happier in their work is much more likely to boost
enrolment than expensive film puffs. Cheerful practitioners are better
recruiters than slick advertising copy, by real life example rather than
through exhortation.'

In our survey of what most influenced our trainees in choosing their
first posts, 'word of mouth' feedback about school 'reputation' was one of
the most influential factors.

What we know about what fulfils and what dismays teachers

There are clearly some factors relating to teacher recruitment and retention which are not subject to government control, and other factors, such as teachers' pay, which have to be carefully balanced against other economic, social and political priorities. There is, however, a degree of irony in David Miliband's statement that the government would not do anything which damaged recruitment and retention (*TES*, 9 August 2002). There is a growing body of research evidence which suggests that there is a tension between some of the education policies which are at the heart of government thinking about how to raise standards in education and the degree to which those policies are having a negative impact on teacher supply.

In most recent research into teacher recruitment and retention over the past decade, pay emerges as one of the main factors. Professor Alan Smithers asserts that the government will never be able to say that it has solved England's teacher shortage problem until it is prepared to invest billions in making pay and conditions as attractive as the private sector, a cost he estimated at around £18 billion a year, or the equivalent of 7p on the basic rate of income tax (quoted in the *Guardian*, 27 December 2000). If teachers really are 'our most precious asset' and politicians and policy makers are serious about making teaching one of the three most sought after and prestigious of professions, 'alongside law or business as a highly respected career' (Blair 2002), this might be a good way of demonstrating serious intent.

Most recent research also suggests that pay is not the only significant factor involved in teacher supply. One of the interesting facets of our own research in this area, which focused on the views of sixth formers and third-year undergraduates, was the extent to which their views on teachers and teaching as a career mirrored the findings of research on the views of practising teachers. A survey of recent research in this field and reports on teacher job satisfaction and morale in the national press show that there is a fairly high degree of consensus about what aspects of teaching are currently preventing teachers from finding their work fulfilling and enjoyable and are acting as disincentives to them remaining in the profession. In a sense 'everyone knows' what the problems are. Survey after survey presents similar findings. Although the precise rank order of deterrents may vary from survey to survey, there is little dispute about the main reasons that many teachers are disenchanted with teaching as a career (see, for instance, Kyriacou *et al.*

1999; *Guardian*, 3 January 2000, 7 March 2000; McCulloch *et al.* 2000; NFER 2000; Smithers and Robinson 2000; *TES*, 7 April 2000, 11 August 2000; Ross 2001; Adams 2001; Audit Commission 2002, *TES*, 25 January 2002; Clough *et al.* 2002).

Study of the surveys and reports noted above reveals that the same factors emerge again and again as the principal deterrents to entering and remaining in teaching. Although the 'rank order' differs from survey to survey, almost all the studies point out that as well as pay, the main issues are workload, pupil behaviour, initiative overload and excessive bureaucracy.

There is also a body of research evidence which provides insight into the elements of teaching as a career which teachers find attractive and fulfilling, and which might help to compensate for negative elements of the job (see, for example, Cockburn 2000; *TES/DFS* 2002; Hutchings *et al.* 2002). These findings are referred to in subsequent chapters.

The problem of correlations and unintended outcomes

The volume of evidence about, in particular, what teachers find off-putting about their conditions of work raises the question of why the government has not been quicker to respond to these concerns, given their public protestations of the importance of a high-calibre, well-motivated teaching force. One of the third-year undergraduates in our survey who had decided against going into teaching explained that 'teachers are not paid enough to put up with all the crap'. Given that teacher supply and retention appears to be about working conditions and teacher autonomy as well as pay, to what extent is it possible to get rid of 'the crap'? Exactly what is 'the crap' and to what extent is it an integral and essential part of teaching in the UK today?

To what extent is a reduction in bureaucracy compatible with the government's strategies for 'delivery' from the centre, and the 'rollout' of strategies, and to what extent can teacher autonomy and creativity be reconciled with the increasing number of government strategies? Target-oriented policy makers and politicians who have to present a positive picture of their achievements are not always alert to unintended outcomes and to the differences between causes and correlations. Thus, any improvements in educational outcome have been attributed directly to the government's main policy initiatives of the past few years, notably league tables, the introduction of the literacy and numeracy strategies, the Ofsted inspection regime and increases in assessment and testing. In spite of teacher scepticism in some of these areas, they have been declared 'non-negotiable' by education ministers and the DfES (Barber 2002; Miliband 2003; Clarke 2003; DfES 2003). Given that much of the recent research literature suggests that some of these policies may be contributing to teacher disaffection, this creates a major problem for schools trying to find ways of improving their supply of high-quality teachers and hanging on to the ones that they have got.

If the government is serious about addressing the current problems of teacher supply and quality, it may have to make difficult choices between its desire to manage and assess educational outcomes from the centre and its ability to respond to evidence about teacher morale and job satisfaction. But in the meantime, what can schools do?

School effect

Both in terms of appointing and retaining staff and in the ways in which they run their schools, heads have to 'play the hand they are dealt', in the sense of making the best of what is available and working within a range of frameworks laid down by central government. We are aware that schools and headteachers are not free agents and that they have to work within the constraints which policy makers impose, but they still have a substantial influence on the ways in which government policy and direction is 'mediated' and translated into within-school practice, systems and culture (see, for instance, Hargreaves 1995; Lawton 1997).

Ingersoll (2001) argues that the organisational characteristics of schools and the ways in which teachers work with each other within schools are important determinants of teacher turnover. This becomes particularly important as schools are urged to move towards systems of self-review, self-evaluation, internal monitoring, audit and target setting. In attempting to be rigorous, effective and 'leading-edge', to what extent might this replicate the pressure and tension of external Ofsted inspection and lead to an atmosphere of 'internal' surveillance and policing? This is one of several areas where heads and senior management teams have to face delicate and complex choices and tensions in terms of how they run their schools. Although the problem of teacher recruitment and retention is widespread and subject to regional and demographic influences, there is also a substantial variation in staff turnover between schools with similar profiles. The recent survey of six London boroughs (Hutchings et al. 2002) found that 'turbulence rates' varied from over 60 per cent to under 10 per cent. Although some schools were clearly facing more difficult circumstances, which would help to explain high staff turnover, there were also factors involved which were not simply attributable to differences in pupil intake. A survey by Hutchings *et al.* (2002) found that issues related to school management were the most frequently cited reason for leaving a teaching post – identified by 45 per cent of leavers. Our own research suggests that in spite of the limits placed on school autonomy by central government directives, teachers and trainee teachers have clearly discernible views on what 'school' factors make their professional lives enjoyable and fulfilling or otherwise (see Chapters 2 to 4).

Although it is true that many teachers have some reservations about the effects of Ofsted inspections, league tables, SATS, the 'rollout' of strategies and the amount of bureaucracy in schools, these things are only part of the quality of their working lives. Making sure that schools are responsive to teachers' professional concerns and to the aspirations of trainee teachers, and making it possible for teachers to enjoy the elements of the job that made them want to go into teaching in the first place, can make a big difference to whether teachers want to work in a particular school, stay working there, or move on.

Notes

1 We are grateful to Dr Simon Everett for bringing this quote to our attention.
2 Recent controversy over school funding puts this last statement in doubt (see, for example, *TES*, 18 April 2003; *Guardian Education*, 22 April 2003).
3 Some respondents said that 'heavy pressure' was applied by the DfEE to discourage schools from resorting to the expedient of a four-day week to cope with teacher shortages, but were reluctant to speak 'on the record'.

References

Adams, C. (2001) 'You can get the staff', *Guardian*, 11 September.
Arnold, J., Cooper, C. and Robertson, I. (1991) *Work Psychology: Understanding Human Behaviour in the Workplace*, London: Financial Times/Pitman Publishing.
Audit Commission (2002) *Recruitment and Retention in the Public Sector*, London: Audit Commission.
Barber, M. (2002) *TES*, 4 October.
Blair, T. (2002) Quoted in 'Bright students deterred from teaching career', *Guardian*, 1 January.
Bracey, G. (2002) 'About that teacher shortage', *Phi Delta Kappan*, 84, 4: 331–4.
Clarke, C. (2003) Speech to NAS/UWT Conference, Bournemouth, 24 April.
Clough, J., Dalton, I. and Trafford, B. (2002) *What's It All About?*, London: SHA.

Cockburn, A. (2001) 'Elementary teachers' needs: issues of retention and recruitment', *Teaching and Teacher Education*, 16, 2: 223–38.

Cockburn, A., Haydn, T. and Oliver, A. (2000) *Why not Teaching*, Research Report for CfBT.

Csikszentmihalyi, M. (1992) *Flow: The Psychology of Happiness*, London: Rider.

DfEE (1998) *Teachers: Meeting the Challenge of Change*, London: DfEE.

DfEE (1999) 'Written evidence to the school teachers' review body', online: http://dfee.gov.uk/tpr

DfEE (2000) *Statistics of Education (teachers)*, table 6, London: DfEE.

DfEE (2001) *Press notice 2001/0061*, London: DfEE.

DfES (2003) Quoted in 'Teachers union to order vote on tests boycott', *The Times*, 21 April.

Doyle, J. (2000) *New Community or New Slavery? The Emotional Division of Labour*, London: Industrial Society.

Groves, P. (2001) 'Recruitment crisis spreads', *Managing Schools Today*, 11, 2: 23–4.

Hargreaves, D. (1995) 'School culture, school effectiveness and school improvement', *School Effectiveness and School Improvement*, 6, 1: 23–46.

House, E. (2000) 'An error theory of educational policymaking', in H. Altricher and J. Elliott (eds), *Images of Educational Change*, Buckingham: Open University Press, 13–19.

Howson, J. (1999) 'Whatever happens to trainee teachers', *TES*, 19 February.

Howson, J. (2000) 'Fewer teachers return', *TES*, 12 November.

Howson, J. (2002a) 'Target time in short supply', *TES*, 6 September.

Howson, J. (2002b) 'London trainees tired of teaching', *TES* 19 April.

Howson, J. (2003) quoted in 'Bursaries help attract new trainees', *TES*, 4 April.

Hutchings, M., Menter, I., Ross, A. and Thomson, D. (2002) 'Teacher supply and retention in London – key findings and implications from a study of six boroughs in 1998–9', in I. Menter, M. Hutchings and A. Ross (eds) *The Crisis in Teacher Supply*, Oakhill, UK: Trentham, 175–206.

Ingersoll, R. (2001) 'Teacher turnover and teacher shortages: an organisational analysis', *American Educational Research Journal*, 38, 3: 499–534.

King, C. (2000) 'Teacher dearth is global', *TES*, 11 August.

Kyriacou, C. and Coulthard, M. (2000) 'Undergraduates' views of teaching as a career choice', *Journal of Education for Teaching*, 26, 2: 117–26.

Kyriacou, C., Hultgren, A. and Stephens, P. (1999) 'Student teachers' motivation to become a secondary school teacher in England and Norway', *Teacher Development*, 3: 373–81.

Lawton, D. (1997) 'Values and education: a curriculum for the 21st century', paper presented at Values and the Curriculum Conference, Institute of Education, University of London, 9 April 1997.

McCulloch, G., Helsby, G., and Knight, P. (2000) *The Politics of Professionalism: Teachers and the Curriculum*, London: Continuum.

McKernan, E. and Taylor, I. (2002) 'Getting schools into focus – school placements and recruitment', in I. Menter, M. Hutchings and A. Ross (eds), *The Crisis in Teacher Supply*, Oakhill, UK: Trentham, 7–27.

Menter, I. (2002) 'Introduction', in I. Menter, M. Hutchings and A. Ross (eds), *The Crisis in Teacher Supply*, Oakhill, UK: Trentham, 1–6.

Miliband, D. (2003) 'Getting to grips with behaviour and workload', *Think Teaching*, (Spring), London: DfES.

NFER (2000) *Who would be a Teacher? A Review of the Factors Motivating and Demotivating Prospective and Practising Teachers*, Slough: NFER.

OECD (1974) *Recent Trends in Teacher Recruitment*, Paris: OECD.

Ofsted (2002) 'Teacher recruitment and retention', online, www.ofsted.gov.uk.

Penlington, G. (2002) 'Who returns to teaching? The profile and motivation of teacher returners', in M. Johnson and J. Hallgarten (eds), *From Victims to Agents of Change: The Future of the Teaching Profession*, London: IPPR, 41–64.

Pollard, A. (2001) 'Possible consequences of strong constraints on teachers and pupils; some fuzzy generalisations from the PACE Project', *Research Intelligence*, 75: 20–4.

Posner, Y. and Tikly, C. (2002) 'Teacher supply and retention in London: the case of mathematics', in I. Menter, M. Hutchings and A. Ross (eds), *The Crisis in Teacher Supply*, Oakhill, UK: Trentham, 207–42.

Ross, A. (2001) 'The Teachers' Supply and Retention Project', paper presented at IPPR seminar 'The future of the teaching profession' London, IPPR, 27 April.

Smithers, A. and Robinson, P. (2000) *Attracting Teachers: Past Patterns, Present Policies, Future Prospects*, CEER, Liverpool: Carmichael.

TES/DFS (2002) 'Survey of teacher lifestyle and morale', 1 February: 1, 4–5.

Wragg, T. (2000) 'No one forgets a waste of cash', *TES*, 23 June.

Chapter 2

What do job seekers want?

In Chapter 1 we explored the context of recent concerns about the recruitment and retention of high quality teachers. Once in the profession, people can discover for themselves the pros and cons of teaching as a career. But how do sixth formers and university leavers view the profession in the first place? Do their perceptions in any way match the realities of the job or is there such disparity that they are doomed to disappointment should they embark on a career in teaching? More broadly, what do young people consider when making career choices and what, if any, implications might this have for the teaching profession?

This chapter is based on a large-scale survey of 1,675 school leavers spread across ten local education authorities and 346 final year undergraduates from nine universities in England. We conducted it in conjunction with our colleague, Ann Oliver, and we gratefully acknowledge the financial support of the Council for British Teachers (Cockburn et al. 2000). The work originated from our earlier work on teacher stress (Cockburn 1996) and teacher retention (Cockburn et al. 2000), together with a wide array of work on careers in general (Argyle 1987; Csikszentmihalyi 1992; Arnold et al. 1998) and teaching in particular (Nias 1981, 1989; Avi-Itzhak 1988; Rodgers-Jenkinson and Chapman 1990; Borg et al. 1991; Evans 1992, 1998; Kloep and Tarifa 1994; Chaplain 1995; McManus 1996). Without going into a long diversion into the merits and shortcomings of questionnaires, we fully recognise that they are considerably less detailed and personal than interviews. Moreover, as you will see in Appendix 1, most of the questions were closed, thus limiting the choice of possible responses. These points notwithstanding, it is important to recognise that the questions were designed on the basis of earlier research, that they were fully piloted and that the use of a survey enabled us to uncover some of the thoughts of far more people than an interview study. Towards the end of this chapter, however, we will discuss the findings in relation to our more in-depth studies discussed throughout this book.

Critical factors in selecting a job

On being presented with 21 factors which might influence their career choice, the largest group of potential job seekers (17.9 per cent) considered that high potential earnings was the most important factor in their selection of career. In contrast, 9.9 per cent stated that a good starting salary was the most important factor for them. In the past – as Lortie wrote in 1975 – it was recognised that a career in teaching did not have high earning potential with respect to the starting salary,

> Income profiles of teachers today are predictable, comparatively unstaged (i.e. increments are small) and 'front-loaded'. A beginning teacher knows what he (sic) will earn and can see that long service brings limited reward.
>
> (p. 84, brackets added)

Moreover there was a view that,

> The traditions of teaching make people who seek money, prestige or power somewhat suspect.
>
> (Lortie 1975: 102)

Nowadays, as people become increasingly aware of government initiatives to both extend the salary scale for teachers and reward merit, possible concerns regarding high potential earnings may diminish. One would hope so, for the results of our survey – conducted in 2000 – showed that pay was the principal deterrent to teaching as a career for 48 per cent of respondents at that time.

Intellectual challenge was the most important factor influencing the career choice of slightly more than one in ten of our 2,011 respondents, making it the second most chosen factor in career choice. A significant minority (32 per cent) of all those surveyed, however, did not think you needed to be clever to be a teacher. Only 11 per cent strongly agreed that 'you need to be clever to be a teacher'. Recent advertisements suggest that teachers are multi-talented but, of the many requirements listed, intellectual prowess never seems to be one of them.

The above raises two particularly important issues. The first is did those seeking intellectual challenge as a priority in their future careers consider teaching as a possible option? Seemingly 53 per cent of respondents did, which is encouraging until one discovers that, of those, 66 per cent subsequently rejected the notion. Of particular relevance in this context, however, is that 27 per cent were still contemplating the idea of teaching as a possible career, suggesting that there might be a window of opportunity for recruiters here.

The second issue is to consider whether teaching is a career which provides intellectual challenge. The answer is multifaceted and, in our view, critical if one is seriously interested in education rather than simply training. There is no doubt that teaching can be a very boring occupation. One of us – Cockburn – is ashamed to admit that she has been bored as a teacher. She has also been taught by bored teachers: on at least two occasions she has had teachers read directly from books as they endeavoured to teach her statistics – first, as an undergraduate and then, later, as a Master's student. She has also watched rather too many bored student teachers trudge through lessons on teaching practice – they, we should report, either changed their practice significantly after her visit or opted not to teach after all. The problem is that, in a variety of settings, teaching need not be intellectually challenging. This has been written about extensively elsewhere (Doyle 1983; Desforges and Cockburn 1987; Marshall 1988; Cockburn 1995) but, in essence, if both teacher and pupils see schooling as an exercise in jumping through hoops, then it can indeed become a dull, routine exercise. Typically, in such situations teachers have a specified set of objectives and, possibly, even a fairly well-defined script. The children – perhaps unknowingly – have their own set of objectives which, in essence, boil down to Doyle's (1983) notion of 'exchanging performance for grades': if they do as required by the teacher, they will be rewarded by praise, a multitude of ticks, a high mark or whatever else might be seen as an appropriate reward.

Such a view is fairly unpalatable for many and, indeed, on hearing it, some teachers rush to deny it. Sadly, however, you will almost certainly have no difficulty in recalling lessons you have seen either as an observer or a participant in which the whole process was almost like a production line (Marshall 1988) with little or no intellectual challenge being demanded of either teacher or pupils. There are, however, notable exceptions to such scenarios. The first is when a teacher truly inspires their pupils and the second is when learners want more from their teacher as in the case, for example, of adolescents who demand to know why they should be in school at all let alone do some work.

Having acknowledged that, in many cases, teaching may not provide intellectual challenge, has it the capacity to do so? Undoubtedly yes

– even when teaching statistics! A recent and good example of this is the introduction of mental mathematics at the start of numeracy sessions in England. Unlike the mental arithmetic – loved by some but loathed by many more – of the 1950s and 1960s, the aim of these is for genuine interaction between teacher and learners and an examination of various possible procedures one might adopt in solving a problem. For example, here is a typical conversation when children are asked the following: 'Sam and Bev had 30 pence and they wanted to buy a bar of chocolate for 70 pence. How much more money did they need?'

RACHAEL: 40p.

TEACHER: Good. How did you do that?

RACHAEL: Well I took 30 away from 70 and got 40p.

TEACHER: Well done. Did anyone do it another way?

JO: I had a number line in my head and I took 10 off 70 and got 60 and then I took another 10 off and got 50 and then I took another 10 off and got 40 and then I took another 10 off and got 30. So I took 4 lots of 10 off and that makes 40.

TEACHER: Great. That's two ways. Any others?

SOPHIE: Well I know 30 and 30 make 60 and then I added 10 more to make 70 so the answer is 40p.

MIKE: I did it like Jo but the other way round.

TEACHER: Can you explain?

MIKE: Well I had 30 in my head and I added 10 and then I added another 10 and then I added another 10 and then I added another 10 and that got me to 70. So I had counted on 4 lots of 10 which makes 40.

TEACHER: Good. Can anyone tell anything about the ways people have been solving this problem?

JACK: Yes. They have all been adding or subtracting.

TEACHER: That's right. Can anyone think of any other method?

SUSIE: Well you could say that half of 70 is 35, take off 5 and you come to 30. 35 and 5 makes 40 so the answer is 40.

RACHAEL: Or you could sort of do like Sophie but instead of adding you could say 2 times 30 is 60 and 10 more is 70 and 30 and 10 is 40.

TEACHER: Okay, let's build on all those ways and see if we can use them when I make it a bit harder. Supposing Sam and Bev had 42p and they wanted to buy a notebook for £1. How much more would they need?

After some initial resistance, it seems that many teachers like the numeracy hour, find it works well even with a class of diverse children and it has increased levels of understanding and attainment: pupils and teachers alike are being intellectually challenged to levels which suit them. Such success stories will no doubt have filtered through to job seekers and, one would hope, encourage them to contemplate taking up teaching and its potential intellectual challenge.

Unfortunately such an incentive runs the risk of being severely hampered by two very powerful forces. The first is the notion that teaching involves considerable paperwork and administration. This has been recognised by the government in England for some time and indeed 41 per cent of our respondents said that these aspects of the job had put them off teaching. The second force is a response to the first: as will be discussed in Chapter 5, increasingly teachers are being provided with ready-planned lessons which clearly lay out what is required of them. This will undoubtedly decrease preparation times but it fails to recognise the crucial need for teacher and pupils to interact and connect if real education is to take place: it is back to the days of reading out of statistics books. No doubt children will learn something from this method (though it may not be as anticipated) but, unless pupils demand more, it is unlikely that teachers will be intellectually challenged by such an approach.

Two other factors that many people considered important when making their career choice were friendly colleagues and job security. Seven out of every ten people surveyed rated friendly colleagues as being a very important factor in their decision-making, and of these 58 per cent had contemplated teaching as a possible career. Half of these individuals had then gone on to reject it as a possibility and 35 per cent were still considering it. These figures are very similar to the overall proportion of those who had considered teaching (56 per cent) and then subsequently rejected it (51 per cent). This suggests that individuals were not swayed more by the friendliness of teachers (or not!) than by any other factor.

Six out of every ten respondents considered job security to be a very important factor in their career choice and thereafter – as with friendly colleagues – the figures were very similar to those of the overall sample, suggesting that job security was not a deciding factor in whether a person opted to teach.

Unsurprisingly, people who had decided to teach were more likely to want to work with children (68 per cent) and help other people (66 per cent) than those who had rejected teaching as a possible career (11 per cent and 31 per cent respectively). What is striking, however, is to compare *the* most important factor in these individuals' career choice.

One in three who had definitely decided to teach put working with children as the main factor influencing their career choice. This contrasts with only 2 per cent who were still thinking about it and a further 2 per cent who had consciously rejected it as a possibility. Of those who never contemplated teaching, fewer than 1 per cent put working with children as their main priority. The differentials were less when focusing on the opportunity to help other people: 17 per cent of those who wanted to teach put it first as compared to 9 per cent still thinking about it, 8 per cent who had rejected it and 5 per cent who had never thought about it. What are the implications of these findings, other than the obvious that, in promoting teaching as a profession, it is essential to emphasise that children are a key aspect of the job!

Who decides against teaching?

Our survey (Appendix I) included asking people whether they had ever considered teaching as a career: 56 per cent said that they had contemplated it and, of these, more than half had subsequently rejected the idea. Here we will consider who these individuals were, what they decided to do instead and the possible implications. As the data for the sixth formers and the university leavers were slightly different, they will be considered separately. As the sample of university leavers – albeit ranged across all subject departments – was fairly small (N = 346), data should be viewed with caution and further enquiry is advisable. They are included here as a discussion point and springboard for further investigation. The number of sixth formers surveyed (N = 1,675) was larger and likely to be more reliable.

One provocative finding is that proportionately more university leavers (i.e. more than seven in ten) had considered teaching as a career as compared to only just over one of every two school leavers. In both cases approximately half then rejected the possibility. This might suggest that careers advisers in universities are more successful in promoting teaching as a career than their counterparts in schools. The difference, of course, may be explained by the fact that many of those advising on careers in schools are teachers themselves.

Table 2.1a shows the top five job categories those sixth formers who had contemplated teaching as a career decided upon instead (N = 443). At first sight it is not unduly surprising, as it could be argued that all the occupations involve skills that are also required by teachers. Having said that, it is a fairly diverse range of occupations and they are not all obviously people-centred as one might predict. The data become more

Table 2.1a The top five career choices chosen by school leavers who have consciously rejected teaching

Career choices	%
1 Healthcare	13.5
2 Art & Design	7.0
3 Business & Management	6.1
4 Media & Marketing	5.9
5 Legal Careers	5.6

Table 2.1b The top five career choices chosen by school leavers who have never contemplated teaching

Career choices	%
1 Healthcare	10.1
2 Art & Design	8.3
3 Legal Careers	6.0
4 Media & Marketing	5.7
5 Engineering	5.2

curious when compared to that in Table 2.1b: these are the top five careers chosen by sixth formers who have *never contemplated teaching* (N = 770).

The similarity between Tables 2.1a and 2.1b is striking, particularly when one appreciates that the data were categorised into 31 different career types ranging from 'careers at sea' to 'animal care' and 'accountancy'.

Rather than targeting a wide spectrum of people in advertising campaigns for recruiting teachers, might the money be better spent and the effort be more appropriately focused if a smaller group of youngsters were considered, i.e. those thinking about careers such as presented in Table 2.1a?

Table 2.2a shows the top five careers chosen by undergraduates who have consciously rejected teaching (N = 117).

Comparing Table 2.2a with Table 2.2b you will note that there are certain similarities, although there some interesting differences between them and those for school leavers. The difference in the prominence of scientific and laboratory work is particularly noteworthy.

Table 2.2a The top five career choices chosen by undergraduates who have consciously rejected teaching

Career choices	%
1 Scientific & Laboratory	10.3
2 Media & Marketing	10.3
3 Business & Management	8.5
4 Art & Design	6.8
5 Banking & Financial Services	6.0

Table 2.2b The top five career choices chosen by undergraduates who have never contemplated teaching

Career choices	%
1 Scientific & Laboratory	13.4
2 Banking & Financial Services	8.2
3 Art & Design	6.2
4 Healthcare	5.2
5 Construction	5.2

What puts people off teaching as a career?

In this section we will consider which factors put people off teaching as a career, looking in particular to see if there are any differences between deterrents for those who still opt for teaching, those who decide against it and those who had never considered it.

Figure 2.1 shows the main deterring factors given by more than 5 per cent of people. Thus, for example, of those who had decided to teach, the most chosen factor which put them off the idea was the perceived levels of stress in the profession (11 per cent). In contrast, pay was the factor which the largest number of individuals in all the other groups selected. This comes as no surprise and is well known among the paymasters.

What is particularly relevant here are the factors which may not be so well acknowledged and appeared to deter all groups, namely the perceived levels of stress in the profession and concerns over the need to control difficult pupils. As discussed elsewhere in this book, there are ways in which to reduce stress in the profession and, indeed, we ignore them at our peril. These data also emphasise that the image of teaching

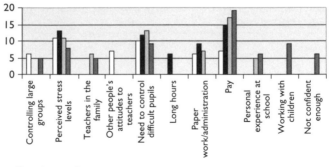

☐ Opted to teach
■ Still thinking about teaching
☐ Decided not to teach
■ Never contemplated teaching

Figure 2.1 The main factor which put an individual off teaching as a career by commitment to teaching given as a percentage if at least 1 in 20 so responded

needs to change: although some may seek stress in their career (it need not, after all, necessarily be negative), clearly a significant number do not wish to teach for the very reason that they *perceive* teaching as a stressful occupation.

One in ten of the respondents – distributed fairly evenly across the groups – reported that the factor which put them off teaching the most was the possibility of having to control difficult pupils. We suspect that, to some extent, this may be due to the current, often rather negative, images of young people which portray them as aggressive, self-centred and over-opinionated. This notwithstanding, Cockburn (1996) noted that when she asked her 'postgraduate students what they were most anxious about as they were about to embark on their teaching career, almost without exception they said "*control and discipline*". Interestingly none of the many experienced teachers I spoke to saw it as a major issue' (p. 38).

One of the main reasons we believe that experienced teachers do not find pupil management a major issue is because they have developed techniques for spotting potential problems and nipping them in the bud. Many of them have also learnt how to teach pupils in interesting and stimulating ways such that misbehaviour is less of a necessity for providing entertainment value. It was suggested earlier that many career seekers are looking for intellectual challenge in their future

Table 2.3 Individuals' commitment to teaching as a career, given as a percentage of those with teachers in their family

	% with teachers in their family	% with no teachers in their family
Opted to teach	42	58
Still thinking about teaching	40	60
Decided not to teach	44	60
Did not contemplate teaching	34	66

jobs – devising strategies for the above certainly can provide such a challenge!

Table 2.3 and Figure 2.1 also reveal some other findings which may be worthy of further research. First, although individuals across all groups had teachers in the family, more than one in twenty of those who decided not to teach were principally put off by their relatives. None of those who opted to teach were so deterred, although 42 per cent of them had members of the family in the profession (see Table 2.3).

It is also worth noting that there was considerable similarity between people's views on the jobs whether or not they had teachers in their families (see Tables 2.4 and 2.5)

Second, at least one in twenty of those who consciously rejected teaching or had never contemplated it were put off by personal experiences at school. For the purposes of this book we suggest that perhaps when placing recruitment advertisments there needs to be more of an emphasis on how teaching has both changed and, at the same time, provides opportunities for people who might wish to change education for the better! More generally, we find it disturbing that so many had such a negative response to their schooling.

Table 2.4 Respondents' views on whether most teachers have time for hobbies given as a percentage by whether they have teachers in their family

		Most teachers have time for hobbies			
		Strongly agree %	Agree %	Disagree %	Strongly disagree %
Teachers in family?	Yes	8	59	29	4
	No	8	64	25	3

Table 2.5 Respondents' views on whether teachers have high status given as a percentage by whether they have teachers in their family

		Teachers have high status			
		Strongly agree %	Agree %	Disagree %	Strongly disagree %
Teachers in family?	Yes	4	35	52	9
	No	3	41	50	6

Before closing this section, it is interesting to note that only 0.6 per cent considered that television and newspaper coverage was the main factor putting them off teaching as a career, although 11 per cent said that it had been at least partly responsible.

Views on teachers and teaching

Before considering how teaching and the teaching profession might be promoted, we will take a closer look at the respondents' views on both the professionals and the profession.

A first glance at Table 2.6 suggests that teachers and teaching come out pretty well in terms of image. Most see teachers as hardworking, enjoying their jobs, deserving their holidays, not isolated but working as part of a team although, as has been said many times before, poorly paid. Teaching is seen as hard work but allowing time for hobbies and as a job for people who know what they want to do. A recent MORI poll (*Daily Telegraph*, 2001) found that 80 per cent of graduates described teaching as hard work.

A closer look reveals that a significant minority – approximately one-third – do not think you need to be clever to be a teacher and slightly more (37 per cent) do not see teaching as a particularly secure job. The latter figure is likely to be subject to quite a bit of variation depending on the job market at the time but, nevertheless, it is something of which to be aware.

More worrying is the view that more than one in three did not think you need to be clever to be a teacher. We believe that to be a good teacher you need to be clever – our survey suggests that more could be done to promote the notion that teachers are intelligent! (The data may also reflect the intellectual quality of the respondents' teachers, which is also disturbing.)

Table 2.6 Respondents' views on teaching and the teaching profession given as percentages

	Strongly agree %	Agree %	Disagree %	Strongly disagree %
Most teachers work very hard	24	66	8	2
Teaching is easy	2	7	63	28
Most teachers have time for hobbies	8	62	27	3
Teaching is enjoyable	8	64	22	6
Most teachers deserve their holidays	34	54	9	3
Teaching is for people who cannot think what else to do	4	9	41	46
You need to be clever to be a teacher	11	56	28	5
Teaching is a secure job	9	54	34	3
Teachers are poorly paid	20	49	27	4
Teachers deal with children who are difficult to control	25	61	12	2
Teachers are high status	3	39	51	7
Teachers must deal with violence	9	60	28	3
Teachers are bossy	8	40	48	4
Teachers are isolated	4	24	65	7
Teaching is about team work	26	56	15	3

Teacher status is also an issue which requires attention, with well over half the respondents suggesting that teaching is not a high-status occupation.

Finally, as discussed above, when considering other data, a significant number of people (86 per cent) think that teachers have to deal with children who are difficult to control and two in three respondents think that teachers have to deal with violence. Similarly, a TTA/NUT survey (1998) reported that 60 per cent of respondents said that the factor most likely to put them off teaching as a career was misbehaving pupils. Given these strong views, it is not surprising that people are put off the profession!

Minorities and the teaching profession

Attracting men and ethnic minorities in sufficient numbers to teaching has long been a problem. Every year the Teacher Training Agency

Table 2.7 Percentages of men and women and their thinking on teaching as a possible career for them

		Men %	Women %
Have you considered teaching as a career?	Yes	5	10
	Yes and it is still a possibility for me	18	20
	Yes but I have decided against it	22	33
	No	55	37
	No	804	1,162

asks how we, as an institution, will attract more of the under represented into the profession. Table 2.7 shows the relative numbers of men and women considering teaching in our study.

The table shows that only one man for every two women intended opting for teaching, which is higher than one would expect looking into staffrooms across the country. Of these men one in every five was hoping to train as a primary teacher, while the remaining 80 per cent planned to teach older children.

We were surprised by the number of men in our sample who seemed keen to teach and suspect that the TTA/NUT survey (1998) of 1,095 16 to 19-year-olds might point a more accurate picture with two in every five girls wanting to go into teaching and slightly fewer than one in every ten boys. Indeed they report that 'of all the careers identified, teaching/education showed the highest gender difference' (p. 2).

Looking at the main factors which deterred men and women from teaching:

- 3.6 per cent of women were put off by having to teach a subject to exam level as compared to 1.5 per cent of men.
- 6.8 per cent of men were deterred by the long hours in contrast to 3.7 per cent of women.
- 20.5 per cent of men were put off by the pay but this was true of only 13.5 per cent of women.

Other than that the figures for both sexes were remarkably similar when it came to deterrents. Looking at the main factors which individuals sought in a career, given the above, it is not surprising that men were more interested in good starting salary (13.7 per cent) and high potential earnings (24.2 per cent) than women (7.5 per cent and 13.7 per cent respectively). Other notable differences were that women were keener to have jobs helping others (10.2 per cent as compared to 3.8 per cent of men) and working with children (6.1 per cent as opposed to 0.6 per cent of men). The final factor which showed any marked differences between the sexes was that the men (2.7 per cent) were more anxious to exert power in their jobs than women (0.6 per cent).

So those anxious to attract more males into the profession clearly need to think how to lure them financially. We are not so sure about emphasising the power they might have.

Before moving on to ethnic minorities it is important to recognise that having few men enter the profession can create problems for those already in it. For example, one male primary teacher reported,

> Although I have always enjoyed teaching here, I realise that I am far happier now that the numbers between the sexes are more balanced . . . There is no homogeneity to our maleness, but there is a certain sense of solidarity born out of our relatively large number. None of us find ourselves sitting around like a spare part, trying to fit in.
>
> (*Independent*, 2001)

Table 2.8 Thoughts on teaching as a career possibility given by ethnic group

| | Q10 Have you ever considered teaching as a career? Please fill in the circle which applies to you | | | | | |
	Yes, that is what I would like to do	Yes, and it is still a possibility for me	Yes, but have decided against it	No	Not available	Total
Other	4	13	16	29	3	65
Bangladeshi	2	4	4	6		16
Black-African		1	3	15	1	20
Black	2	4	5	9	1	21
Caribbean	1	5	8	23		37
Chinese	7	13	20	38	7	85
Indian	3	6	6	9	1	25
Pakistani	139	330	492	739	17	1,717
White	2	4	9	6	19	40
Not Available	160	380	563	874	49	2,026
Total						

Table 2.9 Factors deterring individuals of different ethnic origins from teaching as a career if ≥ 10% selected the option

	Controlling large groups %	Teaching a subject to exam level %	Perceived levels of stress in the profession %	Other people's attitudes to teachers %	Personal experience at school %	Need to control difficult pupils %	Long hours %	Pay %	Not confident enough %
Bangladeshi		13			13			13	
Black-African			10	15	15			30	
Black-Caribbean			19	24					16
Chinese					14	14	19		
Indian					11	11			
Pakistani	20		16						
White			11		10			17	
Other					15			17	

Table 2.8 shows what the various ethnic groups surveyed thought of the possibility of teaching as a career.

As the figures are fairly low we think it would be misleading to analyse them in any great depth. Clearly further research is required if one wishes to make policy decisions.

Having said that, Table 2.9 yields some interesting data. The Chinese and Indians, for example, seem to be deterred from teaching by completely different factors than Black Africans, Black Caribbeans, Pakistanis or Bangladeshis.

Such findings suggest that more focused advertising might be merited if one is hoping to target specific ethnic groups.

Table 2.10 shows the main factors which different ethnic groups consider important when choosing a career. High potential earnings and good starting salaries seem important to most but potentially noteworthy is the finding that job security was the top priority for more than 10 per cent of respondents of certain ethnic origins. Again this has implications for advertising campaigns.

Promoting the teaching profession

There is no doubt that, over the past few years, the government has worked hard to promote teaching as a profession. Vast sums of money have been spent on celebrities recalling memorable teachers and on strategies to lure former teachers back into the classroom. Indeed, Wendy

Table 2.10 The main factor attracting individuals of different ethnic origins into teaching if given by ≥ 10%

	High potential earnings %	Good starting salary %	Clearly defined career structure %	Job security %	Friendly colleagues %	Intellectual challenge %
Bangladeshi	25	13		13		
Black-African	25	25	15	15		
Black-Caribbean		19				
Chinese	27			14	11	
Indian	20	14		11		
Pakistani	16	28				
White	18					11
Other	20			11	12	

Berliner, writing for the *Independent* announced: 'Teaching has not been so attractive for 30 years' (26 July 2001). Several months later however, David Charter – writing for *The Times* (5 November 2001) – reported that the success of the fast-track teacher programme which was launched with 'a fanfare by the Government in September 1999', was 'disappointing despite the £9.2 million spent setting up the scheme'. At the time of writing a year later, this still seems to be the case across a range of government promotions for the profession.

The data presented in this chapter, together with the work of Kyriacou and Coulthard (2000) suggest that, to achieve greater success in their campaign to recruit teachers, the government needs to, among other things, have greater insight into the nature of the task of teaching and the factors individuals see when making career choices. For example,

> The recent teacher recruitment campaign of the TTA focused on the key message: 'no one forgets a good teacher'. This message addresses two of the factors considered in this study: 'a job where I will contribute to society' and 'a job that is respected'. As neither of these two factors appear in the undecided group's top 10 factors of importance, this campaign may well have been flawed in its focus.
>
> (Kyriacou and Coulthard 2000: 123)

This notwithstanding, some people are giving up highly lucrative jobs to take up careers in teaching,

> Increasingly, the profession is attracting a new kind of recruit: high-flyers from cutting-edge industries, who a few years back would never ever have had schools on their radar.
>
> (Wilce 2002: 4)

The above article describes Carla, an IT consultant, who had been earning £70,000 a year. She intends to teach mathematics and recognises that she faces,

> a huge exercise in 'recalibrating my wallet' . . . Even so, she is convinced she is doing the right thing . . . [saying] I'm looking forward to joining a community and, although everyone says, 'Oh, teenagers. You're brave,' working with kids is one of the big attractions.
>
> (ibid: 4)

The same article also considers Jake who explains how he felt about his previous job with a record company,

> I became very disillusioned with it all. It wasn't challenging. You earn a lot but you work long hours, so there isn't time to spend all that money. In teaching, there's so much you can do. You can be creative, use your ideas, and although there's a strict framework for what you have to teach, there's a lot of room for manoeuvre.
>
> (ibid: 4)

He also explained how he so enjoyed 'helping someone to learn' and the contrast with his previous job,

> You know, in a commercial organisation people pay lip-service to the idea 'we're all a team' and send you on bonding weekends and stuff like that. But you walk into a school and everyone basically wants the same thing. They want the best for the kids.
>
> (ibid: 4)

One of the major challenges in attracting people into the teaching profession is demonstrating the many rewards of the job. The third case study in the *Independent*'s article was Cathy, a 32-year-old who,

> used to have a lot of prejudices about teachers . . . At the end of her very first day's observation at X Primary school, a beacon school in south London, she found her views were already changing . . . and been surprised at how much she found herself 'itching to get involved'.
>
> (ibid: 5)

> One of the obstacles in getting her into school in the first place had been the fact that she had wondered, 'What will they think of me?'
>
> (ibid: 5)

When conducting research on why some teachers enjoy their jobs, Cockburn (2000) noted that although

> it would be inappropriate to generalise from a sample of volunteers . . . data from this study suggest that teachers who enjoy their jobs tend to aspire to being teachers for a considerable time prior to embarking on their training.
>
> (p. 231)

She dismisses the idea of brain-washing but goes on to suggest that perhaps primary school-aged children might experience a range of work-based placements

> so that they can begin to reflect on their personal qualities, needs and aspirations and relate them to the world of work in an informed manner.
>
> (ibid: 231)

It would, of course, be naïve to suggest that one visit to a good school will convert everyone to a career in teaching. A student recently withdrew from one of our most difficult courses to get onto after a month,

> due to the current state of the teaching profession. It appears to me that the increasingly bureaucratic nature of teaching is creating an unrelenting workload. This seems to be crippling the profession, transmitting to low morale and a mass exodus from teaching.
>
> (Anon, personal communication, 2001)

Broadening the picture

Throughout this book we consider a wide range of issues relating to teachers and the teaching profession. Before ending this chapter, however, it is worth pausing to consider Smithers and Robinson (2000), 'Ease of teacher recruitment has a lot to do with salary. Countries like Switzerland, Korea and Germany which pay their teachers relatively well tend to experience little difficulty' (p. 49).

We think the government are at last beginning to appreciate this and that a crisis in teacher supply is forcing them to increase salaries. Although this will help increase recruitment and retention, in our view it is not enough if we wish to provide the best for our teachers and their pupils. We hope we provide sufficient insight into the profession to demonstrate that teaching can be a highly skilled and demanding career which has the potential to be tremendously satisfying. Schaffer (1953) pointed out that, 'Overall job satisfaction will vary directly with the extent to which those needs of an individual which can be satisfied in a job are actually satisfied' (p. 3). Wendy (in Cockburn 2000), a teacher who had a range of jobs concluded, 'I definitely think this job fulfils needs for me that other jobs wouldn't' (p. 228).

Teaching can be a soul destroying job and, without care and sensitivity, all manner of factors can transform it from being a frightful profession to one which is thoroughly rewarding and satisfying.

Concluding remarks

Pulling together strands which have appeared both in this chapter and throughout this book, it is clear that the majority of teachers want pleasant environments in which to work, autonomy, intellectual challenge and, most importantly of all, the opportunity to get on with the job of teaching children with the minimum government interference and further externally imposed changes. Pay is not too serious a problem as long as they have sufficient to maintain a reasonable lifestyle and they are treated as professionals with appropriate professional development opportunities. Paperwork and administration are often seen as an unnecessary distraction. For recruitment campaigns to be more successful, we argue that:

- There needs to be a far greater understanding of teachers, their profession and the contexts in which they work. In particular we need to learn from the many successes and address the – sometimes many – issues which are preventing people from realising their full potential as professional teachers.
- Greater acknowledgement of the complexity and challenges of teaching will, in part, help teachers regain their status but with it must come a recognition that teachers would welcome and benefit from more autonomy and less interference from outside parties who have little understanding of their work.
- Such actions would encourage teachers to become advocates for their own profession.
- Moreover, such enhanced understanding would help promote what teaching really has to offer which, coupled with an understanding of the factors job seekers are looking for, would help attract appropriate candidates to the profession.
- To reduce cost and optimise the effectiveness of the above, we – as Kyriacou and Coulthard (2000) argue – suggest that recruitment campaigns focus specifically on those who are contemplating teaching as a profession and the factors which influence their choice.
- Once people have opted to teach it is important to ensure that their teacher training is appropriate.

To address the final issue one needs to be fully aware of both the requirements of the job of teaching and the skills and attitudes of those individuals embarking on teacher education. (The use of the word 'education' here – rather than the more usual 'training' – is intentional. The latter, in our view, grossly underestimates the task and gives the impression that teachers – like dogs – can be trained to perform certain tasks when provided with an appropriate stimulus.) Anderson (2002) recently conducted a survey of 564 recent undergraduates from the University of East Anglia (UEA) in their third year of employment. She asked them to consider which skills they had had 'a lot' of preparation for at university and how that compared with those needed for their chosen professions. Well over half of the graduates felt that their courses had equipped them with the capacity to learn (71 per cent), the ability to use research skills (69 per cent) and use written communication effectively (61 per cent). They considered that they were far less prepared for working with people (32 per cent), time management (38 per cent), coping with change (25 per cent), flexibility (18 per cent), confidence (34 per cent), leadership/initiative (12 per cent) and self-appraisal (18 per cent). All of these are crucial for a successful career in teaching and yet, we suspect, they are not sufficiently addressed in teacher training courses at the moment. This is another area we consider merits further research.

References

Anderson, J. (2002) 'From UEA to employment', report commissioned by UEA Careers Centre, University of East Anglia, Norwich.

Argyle, M. (1987) The Psychology of Happiness, London: Methuen.

Arnold, J., Cooper, C.L. and Robertson, I.T. (1998) Work Psychology: Understanding Human Behaviour in the Workplace, London: Financial Times/Pitman Publishing.

Avi-Itzhak, T. (1988) 'The effects of needs, organizational factors and teachers' characteristics on job satisfaction in kindergarten teachers', Journal of Educational Administration, 26, 30: 353–63.

Borg, M.G., Riding, R.J. and Falzon J.M. (1991) 'Stress in teaching: a study of occupational stress and its determinants, job satisfaction, and career commitment among primary school teachers', Educational Psychology, 11, 1: 59–75.

Chaplain, R. (1995) 'Stress and job satisfaction: a study of English primary school teachers', Educational Psychology, 15, 4: 473–89.

Cockburn, A.D. (1995) 'Learning in classrooms', in C.W. Desforges (ed.), An Introduction to Teaching, Oxford: Blackwell.

Cockburn, A.D. (1996) Teaching Under Pressure, London: Falmer Press.

Cockburn, A.D. (2000) 'Elementary teachers' needs: issues of retention and recruitment', *Teaching and Teacher Education*, 16: 223–38.

Cockburn, A.D., Haydn, T. and Oliver, A. (2000) 'Why not teaching?', unpublished project report to the Council for British Teachers.

Csikszentmihalyi, M. (1992) *Flow: The Psychology of Happiness*, London: Rider.

Daily Telegraph (2001) 'Graduates "not keen teachers"', 10 August.

Desforges, C. and Cockburn, A.D. (1987) *Understanding the Mathematics Teacher*, Lewes: Falmer Press.

Doyle, W. (1983) 'Academic work', *Review of Educational Research*, 53: 159–99.

Evans, L. (1992) 'Teacher morale: an individual perspective', *Educational Studies*, 18, 2: 161–71.

Evans, L. (1998) *Teacher Morale, Job Satisfaction and Motivation*, London: Paul Chapman Publishing.

Independent (2001) 'Where are all the men?', 15 January, p. 6.

Kloep, M. and Tarifa, F. (1994) 'Working conditions, work style and job satisfaction among Albanian teachers', *International Review of Education*, 40, 2: 159–72.

Kyriacou, C. and Coulthard, M. (2000) 'Undergraduates' view of teaching as a career choice', *Journal of Education for Teaching*, 26: 117–26.

Lortie, D.C. (1975) *Schoolteacher: A Sociological Study*, Chicago: University of Chicago Press.

Marshall, H.H. (1988) 'Work or learning: implications of classroom metaphors', *Educational Researcher*, 17: 9–16.

McManus, M. (1996) 'The need to maintain morale', in V.A. McClelland and V. Varma (eds), *The Needs of Teachers*, London: Cassell.

Nias, J. (1981) 'Teacher satisfaction and dissatisfaction: Herzberg's "two factor" hypothesis revisited', *British Journal of Sociology of Education*, 2, 3: 235–46.

Nias, J. (1989) *Primary Teachers Talking*, London: Routledge.

Rodgers-Jenkinson, F. and Chapman, D.W. (1990) 'Job satisfaction of Jamaican elementary school teachers', *International Review of Education*, 36, 3: 299–313.

Schaffer, R.H. (1953) 'Job satisfaction as related to need satisfaction in work', *Psychological Monographs: General and Applied*, 67, 1–29.

Smithers, A. and Robinson, P. (2000) *Attracting Teachers*, Liverpool: Carmichael Press.

Teacher Training Agency/NUT (1998) 'Perceptions of the teaching profession', a joint survey by the Teacher Training Agency and the National Union of Teachers.

Wilce, H. (2002) 'Rewards of the classroom', *Independent*, education section, 19 September, p. 4.

Chapter 3

What factors influence the quality of trainees' school experience?

Having trainee teachers in school

Schools vary widely in the extent to which they are involved in the training of new teachers. In discussions with one (very successful) school, which was not until recently part of our ITT partnership, or any other form of ITT, the head explained that the school did not consider that teacher education was its 'core business' and that any financial remuneration would not compensate for the amount of staff time that would have to be diverted away from the education of pupils.

This position is, however, unusual and schools not involved in any form of ITT are now the exception rather than the rule. A study by Allebone *et al.* (2002) of the participation of schools in ITT in the London region found that 92 per cent of secondary schools were involved in ITT in some way and 67 per cent of primary schools. The introduction of the Graduate Teacher Programme, together with continuing problems in recruiting in some subjects, would suggest that this figure is likely to have increased since 2002.

The recent diversification of routes into teaching means that many schools now run a 'mixed economy' of ITT students, with involvement with PGCE and GTP trainees, and sometimes with school-based training consortia (SCITT schemes) as well. This may be in part due to DfES pressure, with involvement in teacher education now a condition for most forms of distinctive school status and the extra funding associated with such status, or it may be a recognition of the difficulties involved in guaranteeing a consistent supply of high-calibre replacements for staff who are retiring or moving on.

A survey of secondary heads within our own partnership suggested that this was not the primary reason for engaging in ITT activity. The most commonly cited reason for taking trainee teachers was that it was a valuable form of staff development. Other prevalent responses were that it was good for the 'climate' of the school to have a regular influx of young teachers, that inducting new teachers into the profession was an interesting and enjoyable part of teachers' work and that it was good for staff morale and commitment. The survey suggested that financial benefit was not a primary motive for involvement in ITT. Nor is engagement in ITT a 'cash cow' for university departments of education, with many recording a loss, or at best breaking even, on involvement in initial training. As Allebone et al. (2002: 244) point out, 'the lack of resources to provide adequate funding of all the activities necessary to good quality ITT and the consequent reliance on good will, have all put strains on the system'.

In spite of the limited financial rewards from involvement in initial training, the vast majority of those responding felt that, overall, the positive aspects of involvement in training were worth the cost in staff time and the extra burden of administration involved. This does not mean, however, that involvement in ITT is unproblematic, and several studies have pointed out some of the possible tensions, burdens and difficult choices which can be part of involvement in ITT (Barker et al. 1996; Comiskey and Cotson 1997).

Whatever the scale of the 'collateral benefits' of having trainee teachers in schools, involvement in ITT would seem to be one way of increasing the school's chances of securing its share of good teachers coming into the profession. One London head pointed to an occasion where two outstanding members of a high-achieving history department left within the same month. The fact that the department regularly took four history PGCE trainees a year from a high-quality higher education provider meant that two excellent replacements were secured and the momentum of the department was not disturbed.

These advantages, of course, only accrue if there is a reasonable 'pay-off' for the school in terms of there being a reasonable return of trainees who have undertaken school experience at the school taking up posts and of trainees from the HE provider applying for such posts, rather than taking their chances elsewhere. It is difficult to overstate the importance of the overall quality of placement experience provided by the school in trainee teachers' decision making.

Reputation, reputation, reputation

A substantial majority of the trainees in our partnership stay within the region when they take up their first post and 'school location close to current dwelling' is one of the most prominently cited factors in choosing a first post (see pages 68–9). This bears out the research of Hutchings *et al.* (2002), who found that even in London there are strong tendencies for trainee teachers to take up post in the 'catchment area' of their training institution and for teachers to live within easy reach of their school.

Along with location, school reputation emerges as one of the most powerful determinants of the decisions of new entrants to the profession in choosing where to take up their first post (see pages 68–70). There is also a substantial proportion of trainees who take up employment at one of the schools where they have been on placement, and these situations seem to work particularly well, given that both parties know what they are letting themselves into. School reputation works both ways. Just as there are some schools in which offers of posts are keenly awaited, there are other schools which come with a trainee 'health warning' and which do not consequently reap full benefit from their investment in initial training.

Study of trainee evaluations on the quality of their school experience makes it apparent that there are very different ways of looking after trainees and massive variations in the degree to which trainees find their school placements fulfilling and enjoyable. Given that at least half of trainees' time must be spent in schools, the school environment and the colleagues they work with in schools are the dominant influences on their quality of life on the course.

Consistency in the quality of school-based experience is a problem for most ITT providers (Robinson and Robinson 1999). In our own partnership, year after year, trainees' evaluations of the quality of their experience on school placement indicate that there is a massive variation in the extent to which they have been able to gain a positive experience whilst on school placement. Many are clearly sad to leave the school they have been working in and, according to their evaluations, have found the experience of school placement to be as enjoyable, challenging and rewarding as anything they have done.

Although the experience of most trainees within our own partnership is at least satisfactory, with some redeeming features to compensate for placement deficits and problems, we are aware that for some trainees school placement is the most intensively miserable and depressing experience that has happened to them in their lives thus far. Some keep a 'jail diary' of placement on their bedroom wall, so that they can count off the days until the placement is over; it is one of their ways of getting through the placement. Another is the extent to which trainees keep in touch with their peers throughout the placement period – by email and telephone, by meeting up in the pub on Friday nights, or by going out for meals and 'survival' celebrations. When they do meet up, exchanges of 'atrocity' stories and recounting of best and worst features of placement are a mainstay of conversation. They naturally tend to talk about the very powerful and intensive experiences they are undergoing.

Trainees do compare experiences – they are aware of the 'entitlements' that are supposed to be part of partnership arrangements and there is a very strong 'grapevine' about what schools are like to work in. Just as there are 'cold climate' placements, there are 'dream' placements where all facets of the school experience are positive. Trainees talk to their peers about how much they are enjoying the placement, how sorry they will be to leave at the end of the placement and how much they hope a post will come up in their placement school. Although the experiences of trainees working within a particular school may vary from subject to subject, or mentor to mentor, there is often a clear 'school' effect. (The factors which make up this effect are discussed on pages 54–66).

Headteachers and Senior Management Teams therefore need to have a keen awareness about how well their school systems and arrangements for teacher trainees are functioning: what factors trainees consider to be most important in terms of the quality of their school experience, what factors are most influential in their choice of first post and how the reputation of their school stands in the ITT grapevine.

Scales of involvement in ITT

Schools vary enormously in the extent to which they are engaged with training teachers, not just in terms of how many trainees they take on each year, but also in how prominently the training of new teachers features in the school's 'mission'. In our own partnership, there are examples of schools who take modest numbers of trainees on each of the two secondary placements, yet who clearly invest an enormous amount of care and time in setting up a high-quality system for trainees, with a meticulous professional development programme, superb facilities for trainees and exemplary programmes of mentor development.

There is no strong correlation between the size of schools and the number of trainees that a school takes on. There are schools with over twenty trainee teachers of one type or another, and schools that will sometimes offer just one placement to a PGCE course. Allebone *et al.* (arbitrarily) define a ratio of greater than one trainee to ten full-time members of staff as indicating a high degree of involvement in ITT, and a lesser ratio as indicating a limited degree of involvement. Whilst acknowledging the limitations of this indicator, they point out that 'some schools may take few trainees but be very committed to them and spend much time and effort on their development (or vice versa)' (2002: 247).

Some schools stick mainly to a PGCE model, working with a Higher Education Department of Education, but, increasingly, schools are taking on trainees through the Graduate Teacher Programme and are involved in other school-based training schemes. There is nothing in trainee evaluations to suggest that they have any objection to sharing professional development seminars with GTP or SCITT trainees, or even joining in with the school's NQT induction programmes. Feedback from our trainees suggests that many of them enjoy working in schools which have a 'critical mass' of trainees, rather than having just one or two trainees to work alongside. As in many aspects of working in schools, there are pros and cons to different working arrangements. One of the founding principles of our current partnership was that it should be for all schools in the area and that there should be no discrimination between large schools and smaller schools. There are other PGCE partnerships which either require or express a preference for a school to take a minimum number of trainees in order that there is a 'critical mass' of trainees in each school, but a 'quota' system would not work in areas which have substantial numbers of quite small schools and, moreover, many of the schools which are quite outstanding in terms of the quality of experience they provide for trainees only take two trainees per placement. Some heads have explained their reservations about increasing the number of trainee placements offered in terms of parental concerns about their children being taught by student teachers for too high a proportion of the school year. Others have tried to make a virtue of involvement in ITT, and made a concerted attempt to 'educate' parents into realising that involvement in initial training is one of the best ways of guaranteeing a healthy supply of high-calibre teachers for the school. This has extended to successful applications to become a 'training school', or 'partnership promotion school' to accompany the kudos of other forms of specialist status.

There is no optimum ratio of trainees to pupil numbers. We have small secondary schools (around 500 pupils) that take up to eight trainees per placement and large schools that may only want to take trainees in one or two subjects where they feel that they have particularly talented and appropriate departments. Trainees often express resentment or frustration if the school is not able to provide a reasonably appropriate teaching timetable for them, or seem not to be 'geared up' to providing a coherent training programme. Reservations include not being given a broad range of classes in terms of age and ability, being given what they feel is an unfair number of difficult teaching groups, being 'used' as supply cover as a matter of policy, and the feeling that the school has asked to have a trainee to cover a staffing crisis in a particular department. One very well qualified and 'promising' career changer who had hoped to gain experience as a school lab technician before embarking on a GTP placement reconsidered his plans and did not go into teaching as he felt that the school wanted to 'plug the gap' and get a body in front of a class as soon as possible:

> It became obvious to me within a few weeks that they were just desperate to get me into the front line as soon as possible . . . nice people, and they asked in a charming but persistent way. I was constantly being left with a class to mind. . . . There was no way that the school was in a position to give me a proper course of training. It was an inner-city school with difficult kids, I knew I would just get taken apart.

The important prerequisite from the partnership's point of view is the decision to make a full commitment to the quality of training that PGCE students will receive. Given the current arrangements for PGCE courses of training, this means that close attention needs to be paid to the standards for the award of Qualified Teacher Status (QTS) (DfES 2002) and to the precise nature of the 'roles and responsibilities' that are central to the working arrangements of the partnership. This means that there has to be a commitment to a 'whole school' dimension to trainees' school experience, even if only one or two departments are actively receiving trainees. If schools do not have a rigorous and clearly defined professional development programme for trainees, which complements and shows an awareness of the university-based elements of general professional studies, the partnership can be very vulnerable to the triennial Ofsted scrutiny of arrangements for training. Our recent experience shows that this can be one of the most variable aspects of trainees' experience in schools (see pages 65–6). One of the misconceptions of some schools that have expressed an interest in joining the partnership is that it can be just 'a departmental thing', where a particular department simply works with the appropriate subject tutor at the university and there is no need for any overarching programme relating to whole-school issues and professional values and practice.

For partnerships to work well, university departments of education need to recognise that for schools the care of pupils must always come first and that partnership arrangements must acknowledge this. For their part, schools need to commit themselves to the 'spirit' of partnership arrangements, in the sense of always doing their best to fulfil the roles and responsibilities that are part of partnership arrangements. They need to ensure that the trainees' 'entitlements', as laid down in partnership agreements, are met as fully as is compatible with the best interests of their pupils. This is important because trainees talk to each other and are keenly aware of differences in the ways in which schools provide for trainee teachers.

There can obviously be tensions here, and recent difficulties with recruitment and retention have added to these. 'Teacher time' is currently one of the most precious and stretched resources in the education system. Many of the teachers who would be ideally suited to working with trainees, either as subject mentors or as the tutor responsible for the overall conduct of initial training in the school, are also exceptionally talented in other areas. Our experience suggests that, in particular, the choice of the teacher who will oversee and develop the school's ITT arrangements is crucial and is one of the most important determinants of the quality of the school's initial training programme.

Although the contribution of particularly talented subject mentors is often a feature of secondary trainee feedback on the quality of their school experience, there is generally a discernible 'school' effect in their feedback on the extent to which they have found their school placement enjoyable and fulfilling, and the role of the teacher in charge of arrangements for trainees seems to be a key influence on this.

Scale of involvement in initial training can be measured in terms of the total number of trainees that the school works with per year, or by the application of formulae and ratios of trainees teachers to full-time staff, such as the one indicated by Allebone *et al.*

It can also be measured in terms of the degree of commitment which the school invests in its systems for working with trainee teachers, the extent to which those involved in working with trainees are given the time and support to provide a 'Rolls Royce' experience for trainees and the extent to which the most appropriately talented teachers in the school are working closely with trainees.

Although we cannot share this information with our trainees, we are aware that there *are* variations in the quality of school experience for trainees. There is such a thing as 'the dream placement', where we can feel very confident that any trainee sent to a school will be made to feel welcome on their first visit, will be well supported, where trainee entitlements will be met in full and where even the most accomplished of trainees will be prevented from 'plateauing' in their progress. There are also 'mixed' placements, where, overall, there are sufficient 'positives' to outweigh some weaknesses in provision (for instance, where there is known to be an inspirational subject mentor but where trainee feedback suggests that the school's professional development programme for trainees is 'patchy').

We have to remain aware that a school's first duty is to the pupils in their care and that schools can be desperate places at times, when normal arrangements for trainees cannot function as usual, and it has to be 'all hands to the pump' to maintain the normal working of the school. But occasionally we get worrying feedback, *on a sustained basis*, that the 'spirit' of partnership arrangements is not being adhered to and that trainees are getting a raw deal, or, at best, a 'cold climate' experience. One symptom of such a situation, for instance, is that the trainees are *routinely* being asked to cover for absent staff, even outside their age range or subject. It can be good for trainees to realise what a blow it is to lose a precious 'free' period and to understand that there are times when everybody has to help in any way possible to get through a difficult day, but there is a line which divides such situations and the use of trainees to cover staff absence as an act of policy. Another 'warning sign' is when subject mentors have often not been made aware of the trainees' first visit to the school, with the result that the trainees' initial experience of the school is a rather chaotic and negative one. Other symptoms that all is not well are where there is no coherent professional development programme for trainees, or when such meetings are *routinely* cancelled and when trainees do not get 'quality time', one to one, with their mentor on a regular basis – this is one of the most keenly felt grievances of trainees. Just the simple fact of not being made to feel welcome in the school, and the department, on the first visit can have a devastating effect on trainees' morale, and this is another area where there is a wide range of experience and practice.

We are aware that some schools have a policy of internal school evaluation of trainees' experience on placement, or the partnership has a system where trainees' comments on the placement are relayed back to schools unedited. Whilst this might seem to be a commendable example of transparency in assessment policy, we are aware from the comments of many of our trainees that they are (understandably) cautious about being frank in such circumstances, given that they will in most circumstances need to use the school as one of their references.

'Everybody knows'

We have found that serious problems and overwhelmingly negative experiences for trainees are very rare. Most teachers regard working with trainees as a particularly rewarding and fulfilling part of their work, and give above and beyond what the formal arrangements for trainees involve. The vast majority of schools who are involved in ITT do it, as with all other aspects of running a school, because they want to do it well. Given the high stakes involved, however, and the current pressures on school staffing resources, it can be helpful for senior management teams to have good intelligence on the extent to which and the ways in which arrangements for trainees are functioning well. In many subjects, it is a sellers' market and high-calibre trainees are aware that they will be able to pick and choose which post they take. Whatever the formal mechanisms for communication between the university and partnership schools, and however carefully institutions maintain the confidentiality of trainee evaluations, the power of the trainee grapevine (strengthened by recent developments in communications technology) will ensure that 'everybody knows' which are the dream placements, and what the strengths and weaknesses of schools in the area are in terms of their attractiveness as a first post.

Schools which invest heavily and wisely in providing a high-quality experience for trainees are likely to reap better dividends, in terms of the quality and quantity of new teachers applying to work at the school, than those that simply increase the number of trainees they are working with in order to cope with the current problems of teacher supply.

Factors influencing trainees' views on the quality of their school experience

Given that a school's reputation is such an influential factor on trainee judgements about which posts to apply for and that the PGCE course 'grapevine' is a major source of information on this (see pages 68–9), it is important to understand what aspects of school experience are most influential on trainees' thinking.

The following data were derived from recent end of course trainee evaluations and a small survey of trainees (33 PGCE students) to ascertain which factors were most important to the quality of their working lives whilst on school placement. The results of the survey generally corresponded to the nature of feedback which we receive from course evaluations, tending to confirm what we suspected to be the main influences on the quality of their school experience, but the survey, which asked trainees to rank factors in order of their importance, did provide firmer evidence about which aspects of school experience had most impact on trainees' verdicts.

a) The quality and quantity of help, support, guidance and constructive criticism provided by their subject mentor

This emerged by some way as the most important factor in the quality of trainees' experience on school placement. Analysis of the comments made to accompany the judgement gave a good indication of the qualities and attributes that are particularly appreciated by trainees.

It is not possible to read through the responses from the survey and the final course evaluations without coming to the conclusion that the affective domain of mentoring is right at the top of what is valued by trainee teachers. This is not to say that trainees did not want constructively critical feedback, to be challenged and to be provided with a coherent and rigorous induction into the complexities of teaching their subject, but that they wanted these things within a friendly, supportive, encouraging and sympathetic working environment. It is not *just* a matter of being friendly and supportive, but these are the prerequisites for establishing a situation where trainees can make the most of their potential as beginning teachers. There were criticisms of vapid and vague mentoring and 'just being left to get on with it', but the quality of the professional dialogue over the course of the placement was seen as being principally dependent on good interpersonal relationships with teachers, rather than the degree of 'technical' or pedagogical expertise they possess.

It is not the central purpose of this book to focus on all elements and aspects of high quality mentoring, but feedback from trainees suggests that the *climate* of mentoring – the extent to which the trainee is made to feel welcome, part of the school and given support in the early stages of the placement in particular – ranks very highly in their feelings about their placement. Not all mentors seemed to grasp the importance of the changing role of the mentor over the course of the training year and the move from 'coach' and support to that of the critical and challenging friend (Furlong and Maynard 1995).

> 'In a casual and fairly relaxed way, in the first phase of the placement, my mentor would often bump into me at the end of the day and just ask how things had gone overall. He would also enquire how things

had gone when I had taken other people's classes. It just made me feel that he was genuinely interested in how things were going, and helped me to feel more confident in the early stages.'

'Daily brief talk with mentor in first stages of first practice was very reassuring and helpful.'

'Welcoming atmosphere was extremely important – nice to be told that they're happy to have us because we will bring new ideas to the department.'

'Very important to have a friendly mentor who supports you and behaves as if he/she can learn from you as well as the other way round.'

'Mentor always approachable, always helpful.'

'Head of Department was excellent finding the right balance between specific, constructive and focused feedback and guidance, and space to find out for myself. The help she gave was both rigorous, fair and relevant, and was appreciatively received.'

'The school is wonderful. Both subject mentor and link teacher have gone out of their way to be helpful and supportive. I feel that my time in school is largely dependent on getting on well with my mentor and being committed and organised. I am very lucky; my mentor is a wonderful person and teacher. I have been to parents' evenings and in on SEN meetings and curriculum planning sessions. I already feel part of the school.'

There were also some instances where the interpersonal skills and the personality of the mentor, or the overall disposition of the department, made it unlikely that the placement would be a success. The fact that someone is a brilliant teacher does not necessarily mean that they will be a good mentor. There is obviously the danger that taking comments at face value may overlook the possibility that problems arose from trainee inadequacy, but, in several of these cases we received very positive school and trainee feedback on the other school placement.

'Very disappointing. Staff friendly enough in the main but I've had little support. I often feel lost and much of a spare part. The HOD is not very helpful and seems to resent my presence.

The department is well established, with two experienced teachers who excel in managing extra-curricular activities, but right from the start, there was no obvious effort to help me feel at ease or indication that they were there to support me. In fact it was made very clear to me how much extra work they were being forced to do because of me. No time was ever set aside for me to talk to either of them about how I was getting on.

To sum up, I found both members of the department unapproachable, quite oblivious to any needs or worries I might be having, and very unsupportive. They just do not have the communication skills, personalities or temperaments to support a beginning teacher on teaching practice. Any beginning teacher placed at **** School in the **** department is very much in the position of "sink or swim", and this is not a pleasant or very valuable learning environment to be in.'

'Always too busy.'

'Unfortunately, a very negative impact. He was rarely present in school and when he was, he was embroiled in very negative internal politics, using me as a pawn.'

'Tended to concentrate on the negative. I often felt a burden to her.'

'Irritating, rude, sharp criticism very early on and would criticise without providing help and support.'

'Lack of time given to support me, very little encouragement, "pretend" friendliness.'

'Confrontational personal style which took some getting used to.'

QUESTIONS THAT HEADTEACHERS MIGHT ASK ABOUT MENTORING ARRANGEMENTS IN THEIR SCHOOLS

- Have I got the best possible person in charge of managing the quality of trainees' experience in school?
- How good is the mentoring of trainee teachers in this school?

continued

- How well suited are departments to taking a trainee teacher? Is the situation strong across all departments or variable? Does the school sometimes offer placements in situations where it will be difficult to give the trainee a realistic chance of a positive placement?
- How effective are arrangements for mentor development and training, and for augmenting the mentoring *capacity* of the school?
- To what extent is good practice in mentoring shared across departments? Does the school make the best use possible of inspirational mentors?
- Does the school have good intelligence on how well supported trainees feel, and, if not, how might it best develop such intelligence?

b) The general level of friendliness, acceptance and welcome from members of staff generally

This was the second most influential factor, according to trainee feedback. Several mentioned the impact of the first visit to a school. This is an extract from an interview with a maths trainee on a visit to a school to enquire about possible vacancies (he made the point that the friendly response was evident *before* anyone knew he was a maths teacher):

> It was a real contrast with the school I had been in on first placement, which was rather vast and impersonal. . . . While I was waiting in the reception area for a few minutes, practically everyone who passed by asked if I was being looked after, in a very friendly, unfussy way; there just seemed to be a very friendly 'feel' to the place. Eventually the head passed by and said that he had some spare time and would chat with me informally about the school and arrange for me to have a look round if I wanted.

Comments were not just about the atmosphere in the staffroom, or the arrangements for the first few visits to the school. Other factors mentioned were the disposition of the office staff, the tone and manner of responses to telephone calls to the school, and the extent to which trainees were integrated into social and sporting activities. On one occasion, all four of our trainees who had applied for a post at a school (in a shortage subject) withdrew before the interview because of the unhelpful tenor of telephone contact with the school. Four trainees mentioned the provision of free coffee in the staffroom at break times as a positive feature of another school. Several trainees were very appreciative of the care and time that the school had taken in arranging a mock interview for them as part of their school experience. Some schools sent a friendly and reassuring personalised letter or email to trainees before their first visit. This was commented on very positively by many of the trainees where this had occurred. The findings reinforce those of Ross (2001), who found that 'school ethos' and 'friendly colleagues' featured prominently in what teachers were looking for in a school.

As in other aspects of trainee experience, feedback on this facet of school placement was variable.

'Negative, exclusive, unsupportive, critical and unfriendly.'

'Overwhelming level of friendliness and generous advice (and emotional support). The importance of this cannot be overestimated.'

'Staff very busy, little time to build up good relationships.'

'Some members of staff were openly hostile to student teachers – very defensive of resources and the added pressure on their time. One teacher in particular though was very helpful and made a big difference.'

'These people were my life support system.'

'Excellent: I felt part of a team.'

'The school generally was very friendly and treated student teachers as normal people.'

'Made the fact that it was a difficult school easier to cope with.'

'Generally unfriendly and insular.'

'Can really affect quality of life – staff very cliquey – felt very much on the periphery of everything.'

'Staff were great and this was really important.'

QUESTIONS HEADTEACHERS MIGHT ASK ABOUT THE
WORKING ATMOSPHERE IN THE SCHOOL

- How friendly is the general atmosphere in the school overall?
- What is the climate like in the staffroom? How welcoming and congenial is the staffroom and are trainees integrated into the staffroom and/or departmental offices?
- What arrangements are made for the trainees' first visit to the school? How well organised and thoughtful is their initial experience in school?
- How friendly and welcoming is the school office?
- How easy is it to telephone or email the school and get through to the person you want to talk to?

c) The nature of the classes which trainees are given to teach

This emerged as the third most influential factor in trainees' perceptions of their quality of life on school placement, and raises difficult questions about the extent to which trainees should be 'challenged' by working with classes where control may be difficult. Our own view would be that, if at all possible, trainees do need to be exposed to at least one class which requires them to have to work hard to attain a reasonable working atmosphere. Ideally, it is nice to have schools which can provide some classes where the trainee has to focus to a degree on class management, and others where they can concentrate more on how to teach their subject. It is one of many areas of teaching competence where trainees have to learn how to develop teaching skills by doing it, not just reading about it or being told about it. Those in charge of trainees have to make delicate judgements about the extent to which trainees should be challenged in this area and, often, part of this judgement is determined by the ability and resilience of the trainee. The judgement should also be moderated by the school's circumstances. If the school is really at 'the sharp end' in terms of pupil behaviour, trainees should generally not be *extensively* exposed to classes which would challenge even the most accomplished and experienced combat veterans. If the school is less challenging, it might be entirely appropriate to give them more difficult teaching groups. This balance can also be moderated by the extent to which the school will withdraw particularly disruptive pupils from trainees' lessons, its systems for allowing trainees to send pupils out of the room *in extremis*, and the negotiated balance between the trainee trying to stand on their own two feet, taking full responsibility for the class, and the judicious use of departmental and school systems support. There are very few things in professional life more dispiriting than being in effect locked in a room with 30 or so children not fully under your control. As one respondent noted, 'If pupils are co-operative and interested, teaching is enjoyable. If they are disruptive, teaching is a battle.' There is a danger that if trainees are spending large amounts of their time with classes not fully under their control, they will lose sight of the fact that teaching can be an enjoyable and fulfilling job and look elsewhere, or to a less challenging school environment. On the whole, trainees seemed to accept that they should not be too protected from the realities of teaching, but some felt that they were given more than their fair share of difficult classes for reasons other than the rigour of their training. Some trainees felt that this facet of their quality of life had been handled very adroitly, others less so.

'The pupils' behaviour had the ability to make me feel excellent or dejected.'

'I was aware that I was "protected" from some classes on first placement. This may change on second placement but hopefully my experience to date will help me to graduate to classes that are perceived as more challenging.'

'Generally well chosen. Some difficult classes.'

'Difficult, but generally thoughtfully chosen, and I was well supported.'

'I realise that I benefited from diversity to gain experience in classroom management.'

'It's nice to sometimes be able to focus on teaching history more than just classroom control.'

'I was given a variety of classes, some of them with more severe behavioural problems than others, which was beneficial.'

'The mixed bunch of classes gave me a good overview of school life, but the one or two nice classes really did make up for the awful ones. Year 10 on a Thursday was like living through a nightmare.'

'A good mix.'

QUESTIONS WHICH THE HEADTEACHER OR TEACHER
RESPONSIBLE FOR TRAINEES MIGHT ASK ABOUT THE
CLASSES ALLOCATED TO TRAINEES

- Do trainees have at least some classes where it is possible for them to focus primarily on teaching skills other than behaviour management?
- Do trainees have at least some classes where it is possible for them to regard teaching as an enjoyable activity?
- Where trainees have challenging teaching groups, are there support arrangements in place to avoid protracted extreme situations or trainees feeling left to their own devices in situations which any teacher would feel very exposed?
- Are departments making sound judgements about which classes are allocated to trainees?
- Does the school have feedback mechanisms or 'intelligence' about how trainees feel about the allocation of teaching groups?

d) Support, advice and company of fellow trainees in the school

This emerged, slightly to our surprise, as the fourth most influential factor in trainees' quality of life. It raises the question of whether schools who tend to only take one or two trainees might experiment with larger cohorts in order to make the most of this line of trainee support and morale, but this clearly has to be balanced against other factors – such as only taking trainees in departments which are very positive about having them. Trainee evaluations suggest that there was an overall preference for working in schools which took several trainees rather than just one or two, partly for reasons of peer support and partly because it was felt that professional development seminars were more stimulating and varied when groups were larger.

'This was my lifeline; we commiserated and cheered each other up.'

'Without it I would have died.'

'Vital!'

'Good to discuss highs and lows and share strategies for coping with difficult classes.'

'Kept me going from lesson to lesson, encouraging me that things could get better.'

'Good, though more than one student might have been of value, especially in planning cross-curricular work.'

'Only three others but their company was very important.'

QUESTIONS WHICH HEADTEACHERS AND TEACHERS RESPONSIBLE FOR TRAINEES MIGHT CONSIDER ABOUT NUMBERS OF TRAINEES IN SCHOOL

- Is the school taking the optimum number of trainees? Might it increase the number without jeopardising the quality of trainee experience or alienating staff?
- Does the school provide the maximum opportunity for trainees to help and support each other?
- Where schools take only one or two trainees, do NQTs and younger colleagues provide support for trainees?

e) The effectiveness of support provided by the school system

This was construed largely in terms of support in dealing with pupil behaviour, and nearly all trainees expressed a preference for quite clear and structured systems for dealing with class management issues (unlike teaching approaches, where a degree of autonomy was preferred). It was difficult not to feel that in terms of 'the grapevine', and the impact that this would have on trainees' choice of posts to apply for, this would be a highly relevant factor.

'Important to know that you are supported – if sending a pupil out, detentions etc. This was amply provided.'

'Negatively affected my quality of life. Lack of senior management presence on Friday afternoons.'

'Quite a well run school, despite its problems. Demands a lot of the pupils.'

'Don't feel much respect for upper management.'

'Lack of consistency with reference to discipline across the school. Lack of support from senior teachers.'

'Very good discipline procedure backed up teaching.'

'There was a definite need to follow up on management problems, enforce detentions, etc.'

'Very helpful discipline procedure.'

'Support system clear and well defined.'

'A very clear programme of punishment and school rules is in force but a little more assistance would have been appreciated at the beginning of placement when I was finding my feet.'

'Very useful, clear system which definitely made my life easier.'

'School system for discipline in place but needs to be used by all teachers.'

'The school had very strong support and this was very important.'

'The system is effective and supports the classroom teacher.'

QUESTIONS WHICH THE HEADTEACHER OR TEACHER RESPONSIBLE FOR TRAINEES MIGHT ASK ABOUT SCHOOL SUPPORT SYSTEMS

- How effective are the school's systems for detentions, internal exclusion, etc?
- Is there consistent use of these systems which will be apparent and 'shared' by trainees?

- Do trainees feel able to make use of school systems, with liaison with other colleagues where appropriate?
- How do trainees feel about the level of support which school systems offer?

f) The quality of professional studies seminars and the quality of general help, induction and support given by the teacher in charge of trainees

This was another area where there tends to be a range of trainee experiences. In some cases, trainees spoke very movingly about the help they received from the teacher in overall charge of the ITT programme. There were instances where their support and guidance had been a key factor in enabling them to survive crises and get though the course successfully. There were other cases where the trainees had barely met this person. According to the feedback from trainees, school professional development programmes vary from the inspirational to the non-existent. From the perspective of the university, the Link Teacher/ Professional Tutor does seem to have a consistently important influence on the overall quality of the school's ITT programme.

This is a sensitive area for ITT partnerships – it is not for the university to decide how schools should allocate senior colleagues to key posts, but it can be frustrating when feedback suggests that the Link Teacher is too overwhelmed with other responsibilities to do justice to the job. There sometimes seems to be a reluctance for Link Teachers to acknowledge this and explore other options, by either delegating to someone else or sharing the responsibilities in order to develop other colleagues' experience in this area. We feel that often there is someone on the staff who would be keen to take on the post and throw themselves into it wholeheartedly.

Although this facet of ITT in schools is not viewed as being as significant in the eyes of trainees as the factors mentioned above, it does transmit to trainees a view of how the school approaches the issue of professional development. There is the danger that trainees may assume a correlation between the quality of the school's arrangements for ITT and their approach to staff development more generally.

(Trainee comments on the quality of Professional Studies seminars):

'The best bit of the whole course.'

'These were delivered with enthusiasm and well organised.'

'A comprehensive PD programme, the Link Tutor was always available for advice.'

'PD is non-existent.'

'I had no PD in the entire placement.'

'Hardly had any. Very little support from the School Tutor.'

'Adequate.'

'These are a bit dispirited.'

'Often seems to be slightly shambolic.'

QUESTIONS WHICH HEADTEACHERS MIGHT ASK
ABOUT THE QUALITY OF THE SCHOOL'S PROFESSIONAL
DEVELOPMENT PROGRAMME FOR TRAINEES

- How do the school's arrangements in this area of ITT compare to trainees' experiences in other schools?
- How does it affect the views of trainees on the desirability of this school as a permanent post?

References

Allebone, B., Griffiths, J., Kendall, S. and Sidgwick, S. (2002) 'The participation of schools in initial teacher education in the London region', in I. Menter, M. Hutchings and A. Ross (eds), The Crisis in Teacher Supply, Oakhill, UK: Trentham, 243–59.

Barker, S., Brooks, V., March, K. and Swatton, P. (1996) Initial Teacher Education in Secondary Schools, London: ATL.

Comiskey, B. and Cotson, M. (1997) 'Striking a balance: teachers, tutors and students' views of ITE partnership and quality', Mentoring and Tutoring, 4, 3.

DfES (2002) Standards for the Award of QTS, London: DfES.

Furlong, J. and Maynard, T. (1995) Mentoring Student Teachers, London: Routledge.

Hutchings, M., Menter, I., Ross, A. and Thomson, D. (2000) 'Teacher supply and retention in London – key findings and implications from a study carried out in six boroughs in 1998–9', in I. Menter, M. Hutchings and A. Ross (eds), *The Crisis in Teacher Supply*, Oakhill, UK: Trentham, 175–206.

Robinson, I. and Robinson, J. (1999) 'Learning to live with inconsistency in student entitlement and partnership provision', *Mentoring and Tutoring*, 7, 3: 223–39.

Ross, A. (2001) 'Issues in teacher supply and retention', paper presented at IPPR/IPSE Conference, 'Teacher Supply and Retention: Emerging Issues', University of North London, 12 June.

Chapter 4

What are trainee teachers looking for in their first posts?

We conducted a survey of a sample of our trainees towards the end of the course in 2002 to see what they were looking for in their first post. They were asked what factors were most influential in terms of getting them to make an application for a teaching post and what factors were the most influential in persuading them to accept a particular teaching post. The results are summarised in Tables 4.1 and 4.2.

Apart from school location, by some way the most prevalently cited factor was the reputation of the school in terms of the views of other trainees who had been on placement there. The views of their peers appeared to be more influential than Ofsted reports on schools, although

Table 4.1 What factors were most influential in terms of getting you to apply for teaching posts generally (what were you looking for)?

Factor	Number of trainees citing factor as an influence*
School's location	35
Course grapevine	18
Was on placement at the school	9
School had a sixth form	8
School's Ofsted report	8
Wanted a 'challenging' school	3
Wanted a 'mixed comprehensive'	3
Didn't want 'challenging' pupils	2
NQT on the advertisement for the post	2
Wanted school with good academic reputation	2
Wanted school with technology status	1
Wanted school without sixth form	1
School wanted you to visit	1

* N= 59 (37 secondary, 22 primary trainees)

8 of the 59 trainees did mention the school's Ofsted report as a factor in applying for a post. Where trainees had enjoyed a successful placement at a school, this was clearly an influential factor, and 15 per cent of the cohort surveyed ended up teaching at one of the schools where they had been on placement (this figure may well be an underestimate as the survey was undertaken before the end of the course when some trainees had still not found posts). In the words of trainees:

'The school was my first placement. I knew it had a nice friendly atmosphere and that I would get a lot of support. I also knew I got on well with all the staff. It is also a school with lots of new ideas – and they were happy for me to start in July.'

'I was on second placement there and enjoyed it, plus I thought it would be an advantage in my NQT year to be in familiar surroundings.'

'The school I accepted was the school for my second placement. Although much was not ideal (I would only be teaching 50 per cent of my subject), I had really enjoyed the placement and leapt at the chance.'

'I had enjoyed my first placement there, liked the atmosphere, lots of support, fairly laid back, nice atmosphere. It's a 20 mile journey but I know I'll enjoy it there.'

Considering the fairly high profile of the debate about moves away from 'bog-standard' comprehensive schools at the time that the survey was conducted, perhaps surprisingly few respondents commented on the 'type' of school that they wished to work in, in terms of it being a 'specialist', 'beacon' or 'training' school. One trainee expressed the desire to teach in a technology college, and two wanted to teach at a school with good academic results, but there were also some who wanted 'a challenge', or who wanted to teach in a 'mixed' comprehensive. In the words of one trainee, 'I want average students, a mix.' Another said 'I suppose I don't really want to teach at a school that is special in any way . . . I just want to teach at a bog-standard comprehensive school . . . there's enough to be getting on with without thinking about that.' (Although there was no strong evidence here to suggest that trainees would gravitate to the top tiers in the 'ladder' of comprehensive schools which has been set up by government policy, one caveat here is that

Table 4.2 What factors were most influential in persuading you to accept a particular teaching post?

Factors	Number of trainees citing factor*
Friendly colleagues/good 'feel' to the school (tended to be expressed in terms of friendly colleagues)	39
Good resources in the department/school	21
Felt would be well supported (often expressed in relation to class management issues)	19
Felt comfortable with the nature of the pupils at the school	14
Felt that they would get on with their line manager/head of department	14
Impressed by quality of the school's induction programme	12
Impressed by/felt that they would get on well with the head teacher	8
School ethos	4
Positive impression of the staffroom	3
Provided with laptop computer	3
Would be paid from July	3
Relaxed/ informal interview	3
Impressed by school's discipline policy	2

* N= 59 (37 secondary, 22 primary trainees)

good resources emerged as an influential factor in accepting posts, which raises the question of whether the extra funding generated by, for instance, specialist status, makes a discernible difference to levels of resourcing in schools.)

In terms of what trainees wanted, 'climate' seemed to be much more influential than type of school. The second part of the survey asked trainees to explain what factors were most influential in persuading them to accept a particular teaching post. A summary of the details is given in Table 4.2.

Although many trainees were obviously concerned about the issues of behaviour management that would arise at the school, and the nature of the pupils and groups they would be asked to teach, overall, it would appear that trainees are more concerned about relationships with the 'grown ups' than the pupils. This is exemplified by the response of a secondary science trainee, who took a post at his second placement after a negative experience on first placement which had been less challenging in terms of pupil behaviour:

> Personal and professional relationships are number one in searching for a job . . . Without question the most important reason for accepting a post was due to the fact that I knew the head of department and staff very well. For me, I think the success of teaching is based on the cohesion of the staff at a school. Knowing that you will get on well with the staff in a particular department at both a professional and personal level underpins the reason to accept a particular job. The type of school, its geography and social make up of pupils are secondary to the team who you will be teaching with.

School culture is also part of what seems to influence trainees' judgements on the 'feel' of the school, with a picture emerging of a preference for friendly, relaxed and collegiate environments, where staff worked together to support each other in dealing with the challenges of dealing with challenging pupil behaviour:

> Initially very impressed by the school, the facilities and the behaviour of the pupils. Gradually, over the placement I began to feel it wasn't the sort of school for me. It was heavily results focused and had a definite top–down management structure. My second school was much smaller, the pupils much livelier – which strange as it may sound, I loved. The staff were very supportive and had more time for you. There were more opportunities available in this school in terms of the flexibility in the school and involvement in other curriculum areas.

There was also sometimes an issue in terms of the tensions between teacher autonomy and leadership and support, as exemplified by this response:

> Not just left alone to get on with it, but confident in you to leave you in control, make your own mistakes. One of my teaching placements in the PGCE year was very structured, and it made me think that you wanted to have at least some autonomy, professional choices to make,

I preferred it when there was a more independent style. Now I feel that there is a happy medium, with some structure but room for manoeuvre.

The personality of the person leading the department . . . A department with strong leadership, very definite aims on language and literacy, those first two years in secondary school are so important, and the feeling that you can make a difference by how you approach that challenge. Leadership but an open relationship, give and take, compromise, agreement to make the best of things, someone I think I can learn from. The literacy strategy can be prescriptive, but it depends on the way it's handled.

Although there were some trainees who expressed a preference for working in schools which were quite difficult in terms of pupil behaviour, and definitively wanted to work in a challenging inner-city comprehensive, for many trainees, pupil behaviour was an issue, and trainees sometimes demonstrated a healthy self-awareness of their strengths and weaknesses. One secondary trainee was strongly urged to take an opportunity which had arisen where she had been on her school placement:

They were incredibly nice, and I could tell that they really wanted me to take the job; I felt bad saying no but I know from my experiences during the PGCE year . . . I know enough about myself to know that I would not be happy working in a school where there is quite a lot of difficulty getting and keeping control of classes. They were really nice people, and offered lots of support – which I'm sure was genuine and sincere – but, at the end of the day, I just know that I'm not the sort of person who could enjoy that sort of job. I want to be able to enjoy my teaching and not have to battle with class management for most of the NQT year.

In evaluations of their experience on school placement, several trainees expressed a preference for schools and departments where they would be allowed a degree of latitude to prepare and deliver their lessons as they wished, rather than being subject to a very tight degree of direction. In terms of behaviour management however, many of them clearly felt more comfortable where schools had a clearly defined and quite prescriptive system of dealing with class management issues. It was not difficult to find comments such as 'good discipline system' featuring in their evaluation comments, and in group interviews, trainees suggested that one of the advantages of working in 'difficult' schools, including those which were in 'serious weaknesses', or even 'special measures', was that they often had highly structured and very clear and strong systems for dealing with difficult pupil behaviour.

'The main things that make it difficult for teachers to enjoy their job'

A separate survey asked trainees to indicate what they felt were three of the main things that made it difficult for teachers to enjoy their job. The results of their 'first choice' of deterrent to enjoying teaching are given in Figure 4.1.

When we looked at what the responses were overall, for all three factors which the trainees were asked to give, paperwork/bureaucracy emerged as by some way the most commonly cited – mentioned by 171 of the 194 trainees, followed by pupil behaviour (87) and workload (72). Other impediments to being able to enjoy teaching were:

- Poor resources for teaching (34)
- Planning/prescription for planning (24)
- Class size (24 – mainly primary)
- Lack of support (23)
- Policy changes/government policy (14)
- Having to do cover (12)
- Bad publicity/low status (11)

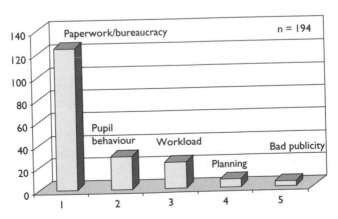

Figure 4.1 First choice deterrents to enjoying teaching

- Ofsted (11)
- Pay (10)
- Parents (9)
- Too much testing (6)
- Targets (6)
- Literacy hour (4)
- Staff (3).

Although 'school' factors such as lack of support in dealing with difficult and disruptive pupils and negative attitudes of other colleagues could be discerned in some responses, comments more often focused on the effect of policy initiatives which impacted on the 'climate' of teaching:

'Jumping through bureaucratic hoops to please outside agencies.'

'Pressure to pass tests rather than to learn.'

'Lack of time to teach non-core subjects.'

'Constant assessment and the feeling of not being trusted.'

'Political directives that compound an already stressful situation.'

'Demoralising tests and initiatives from government, TTA etc.'

'Endless mind-numbing ideas coming down without support money.'

'Ticking silly boxes.'

The most commonly mentioned 'school' factor was the difficulty and frustration of dealing with disruptive pupils. In many cases this was accompanied by a feeling that the senior management team of the school, or 'school systems', were not strong enough in supporting staff in dealing with these problems. Inadequate school resources, poor facilities, problems over photocopying or computers were next in order of prevalence.

Concern has been expressed about the danger of teachers with negative attitudes alienating trainees from the profession. Claxton's study of the main concerns of trainee teachers illustrates this: 'The biggest fear was that they might, as one of them put it, "end up like that". They all knew, without much discussion, what "like that" meant; cynical, bored, boring, burnt out' (Claxton 1989: 4). A study by Adams (2002) of modern foreign language trainees also found that several trainees were discouraged by encounters with negative comments from demoralised staff. In our survey, several trainees indicated that tensions and 'communications difficulties' between members of staff impaired their enjoyment of teaching placement and that cynical or jaded members of staff did not provide helpful role models for those going into teaching, but these amounted to no more than a handful of responses to this question. Even though this does not seem to be the most prevalent of concerns amongst trainees it nonetheless poses the question of how much attention is paid to trying to ensure that trainee teachers work primarily with teachers who have a clear grasp of the importance of the 'affective domain' of mentoring (see pages 55–6).

Teacher morale did not emerge as one of the most obviously influential factors in deciding whether trainees felt that they would 'stay or go'. Trainees' perception of teacher morale in the schools they worked in suggested that most schools were at one of the mid-points in the continuum between 'excellent' and 'very poor' (see Figure 4.2). In only four schools was staff morale described as 'excellent' but, also, in only seven was it described as 'poor' or 'very poor'. Even where trainees had worked in schools where morale was towards the bottom end of the continuum, their determination to continue to pursue a career in teaching seemed relatively unimpaired. The high levels of communication

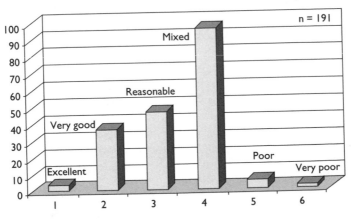

Figure 4.2 Trainees' perceptions of teacher morale

between trainees during the course makes them aware that schools are very different in terms of 'climate' and 'culture', and it seems possible that trainees can stoically endure cold-climate placements in the knowledge that more congenial working atmospheres lay around the corner. Where trainees withdraw from the PGCE course before the end of the year, exit interviews and letters of withdrawal within our own partnership suggest that the most common reasons are that trainees realise from the feedback which they receive that they do not possess the requisite skills and abilities to be effective teachers and that it is 'not for them', or that the overall workload is way beyond what they expected it to be. Many withdrawing trainees mention that disruptive and difficult pupil behaviour does not make it possible for them to enjoy their teaching, but this is also mentioned in other contexts by a substantial number of trainees who decide to go into teaching in spite of this. Sometimes health concerns or personal/family problems lead trainees to withdraw or intercalate. Although there are some trainees who mention negative attitudes to teaching as a contributory factor in their decision to withdraw, or problems and tensions with their supervising mentors, this does not emerge as a dominant factor. There are occasions when trainees who are making good progress and who are felt to be 'promising' or even talented teachers withdraw from the course, but these are a minority. This is broadly in line with the findings of Chambers and Roper (2002) and Lewis (2002), but we have also encountered trainees who have withdrawn citing disillusionment with 'the system', 'the way that education is run', 'lack of autonomy' and aspects of government policy as the main reason for their withdrawal. Some trainees go out of their way in their withdrawal letter to stress that it is not a reflection on the quality of their school experience and that it is 'factors beyond the school's control' that have led to a change of mind about going into teaching as in these examples:

> My decision to leave the profession is primarily due to the current state of the teaching profession. It appears that the increasingly bureaucratic nature of teaching is creating an unrelenting workload . . . I am beginning to understand why 40 per cent of all trainees leave the profession within three years. A major factor must be the pressure that teachers face from both Ofsted and unrealistic target setting. There appears to be a real disparity between government expectations and the reality of the classroom.

Several exit interviews also referred to bureaucracy and workload as the main reason for withdrawal:

They appear to be doing all the wrong things if they're trying to get people to go into teaching . . . it really puts people off . . . the first thing you get is this pile of standards dumped in front of you.

Well, the main reason I'd say is the bureaucracy actually away from the teaching. The amount . . . the workload just seems phenomenal. Another point is target setting that just doesn't seem to correspond to anything in the classroom.

'The main things that provide job satisfaction for teachers'

Trainees were asked what were the main things that they thought helped to provide job satisfaction for teachers and asked to name three factors. The most prevalent responses are shown in Figure 4.3.

Over 200 of the responses related to the pleasure derived from working with children, expressed either in terms of their response to teaching, seeing them make progress in learning, or simply the satisfaction of being in a classroom, working with children. It is perhaps interesting to note that in our survey of sixth formers and third-year undergraduates (see Chapter 2), the intrinsic pleasure of working with young people did not figure prominently in responses, even amongst those considering teaching as a career. Pupils were more commonly seen as a source of

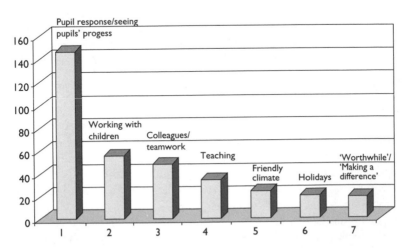

Figure 4.3 Trainees' perceptions of the main things that provide job satisfaction for teachers

threat or anxiety. Perhaps young people who have not had any school experience or observation as a potential teacher or classroom assistant have an insufficiently developed appreciation of the positive aspects of working with children, and more should be made of this in publicity about teaching.

A further 20 responses made reference to the friendly 'climate' sometimes found in working in schools and classrooms, and 49 responses indicated satisfaction in working together with colleagues, with comments such as:

'Comradeship'

'Teamwork'

'Working in a committed team'

'Good team morale'

'Good teamwork amongst staff'

'Team spirit in the school'

The collegial and collaborative nature of teaching and learning in schools is clearly a potentially influential factor in contributing to job satisfaction in teaching, and in our interviews with teachers (see Chapter 5) some schools seemed to have a more developed awareness of this than others. Certainly, many of the recent government initiatives aimed at 'reforming' the profession have tended to focus on individual rather than collaborative performance.

Thirty-five responses spoke of the intrinsic pleasure and satisfaction that could be derived from the practical activity of teaching; 'being able to just get on and teach', in the words of one respondent. A common strand in both trainee and teacher responses was the dispiriting volume of activity which stood in the way of, or was additional to, planning lessons and teaching pupils. 'I love the teaching, it's all the other things that stop me enjoying the job' (young physics teacher who has recently left the profession).

A substantial number of the respondents had significant experience of other employment (104 out of 194), and we have found that an increasing number of our trainees come to teaching after one or two years in other professions which they have not found fulfilling. This is reflected in the

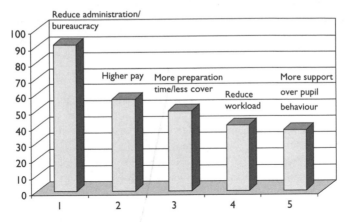

Figure 4.4 Trainees' perceptions of what might be done to improve the quality of teachers' working lives

20 responses which indicated that teaching was considered to be a worthwhile activity and that some job satisfaction derived from the belief that they were 'making a difference' to pupils' lives and life chances; in the words of one trainee, 'a sense of contribution to the progress of the species'.

'Variety' evinced 11 responses, and ten trainees cited involvement in extra-curricular activities as a source of job satisfaction. Helping pupils to do well in examinations was a factor mentioned by eight respondents, and being praised or made to feel valued (either by senior colleagues or parents) was also mentioned by several trainees as something that helped them to enjoy their work.

When asked what might be done to improve the quality of teachers' working lives, the responses reflected many of the concerns outlined previously (see Figure 4.4).

Other suggestions included:

- Reduce class sizes (37)
- More learning support assistants (29)
- Better resources for teaching (23)
- Less prescription (13)
- Recognition (10)
- A laptop computer (5)
- Less change/'hoops' (5)
- More in-service training (4)

Unsurprisingly, comments tended to reflect the factors cited as having a negative influence on the extent to which teaching could be enjoyable and fulfilling:

'More time spent on actual teaching.'

'More time to focus on the actual physical act of teaching.'

'Get rid of Hitler mentality of senior management team. Teachers are not just large kids, so don't treat them like that.'

'A more balanced and realistic approach to inclusion.'

'More effective disciplinary support against disruptive pupils.'

'Stop moving the goalposts.'

'Less unnecessary paperwork.'

'Less pointless constraints placed upon them.'

'Schools and teachers to have more control over curriculum and management issues.'

'Removing education from the merry go round of politics.'

Several of these areas clearly have resourcing implications, but not all of them. What is particularly worrying is that the recent crisis over school budgets (see for instance, *Guardian*, 24 May 2003) has meant that many schools have had to make reductions in some of the areas related to these suggestions for improving teacher morale and fulfilment, such as reduced capitation for departments, cuts in INSET budgets and laying-off LSAs. The responses indicate that it is not just, or even primarily, about teachers' pay.

Will they stay or not? Trainees' feelings about teaching towards the end of their training

As part of the questionnaire survey of 194 trainees towards the end of their training, we asked what they thought they would be doing in five years' time (see Figure 4.5).

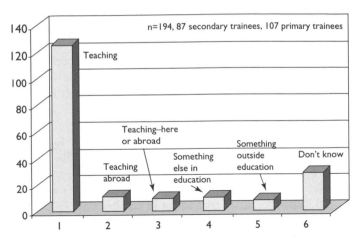

Figure 4.5 What students see themselves doing in five years' time

Although over 64 per cent indicated that they thought that they would still be teaching in this country in five years' time, this includes several cases where this was conditional:

'If bureaucracy improves.'

'Depends what the government does about inclusion . . . I don't plan on living my life with unbearable stress levels.'

'If I continue to enjoy it.'

'Perhaps part time.'

'Tough one, not necessarily teaching, we'll see.'

Over 11 per cent of the sample indicated that they were either planning to teach abroad or considering working abroad as teachers. Given the warnings that competition for teachers is likely to become global over the next decade (see Chapter 1), this is a worryingly high proportion. Of those indicating that they wanted to continue to work in education but not in a school context, the choices varied between working as an educational psychologist, working in museums and galleries, and working in further or higher education.

In terms of career progression, several respondents mentioned going part time, or having a family and working part time. There was little to suggest that substantial numbers of trainees were keen to 'climb to the top of the greasy pole'. Going into school management as head or assistant head did not figure prominently in responses, with only five trainees making reference to any aspiration to becoming part of a school's senior management team. Thirty-five trainees saw themselves becoming heads of department or subject co-ordinators. This was with wide variations according to subject specialism in the case of secondary trainees. Eight out of 13 PE trainees and seven out of 16 geographers hoped to become heads of department in five years' time, but this fell to one out of 25 historians and two out of 15 English trainees. Whether this is a question of differences in levels of ambition or in professional confidence is difficult to say. Similarly, there were no references to becoming Advanced Skills Teachers, but this might be construed as proper modesty in a trainee rather than lack of interest. Several respondents did not mention career progression in terms of promotion, but expressed the hope that they would have become 'better' at the job, and would be enjoying their teaching:

'Being a successful, confident teacher.'

'Teaching more confidently.'

'Working in a school I am well suited to and enjoying it.'

There were over 40 responses which indicated in one way or another that trainees did not know whether they would still be in teaching in five years' time, or that it would depend what happened in the interim period. As with the views of sixth formers and third-year undergraduates noted in Chapter 2, it would seem that there is 'a lot to play for'.

References

Adams, J. (2002) 'The case of Modern Foreign Languages', in I. Menter, M. Hutchings and A. Ross (eds), *The Crisis in Teacher Supply*, Oakhill, UK: Trentham, 87–100.

Chambers, G. and Roper, T. (2002) 'Why students withdraw from initial teacher training for secondary schools: the Leeds experience', in I. Menter, M. Hutchings and A. Ross (eds), *The Crisis in Teacher Supply*, Oakhill, UK: Trentham, 59–86.

Claxton, G. (1989) *Being a Teacher*, London: Cassell.

Lewis, P. (2002) 'An enquiry into male drop out rate on a PGCE primary course at a university college and success indicators for retention', in I. Menter, M. Hutchings and A. Ross (eds), *The Crisis in Teacher Supply*, Oakhill, UK: Trentham, 123–39.

Chapter 5

What do teachers want? The quality of teachers' working lives[1]

The recent crisis in teacher recruitment and retention has led to several studies, both here and abroad, focusing on why teachers become stressed and, in some cases, leave the profession (for example, Evans 1998; Spear *et al.* 2000; Smithers and Robinson 2000). A lesser explored perspective is why teachers choose to stay in the profession and what factors influence this decision, although a recent small-scale study (Cockburn 2000) explored why some teachers enjoyed their job. If we are to improve teacher retention, then it is imperative that we develop our insights into why some individuals remain in teaching in spite of less edifying aspects of the job and in the face of the (well-documented) stresses and strains which are placed on them. The following statistics from an Association of Teachers and Lecturers survey (1998) of 1,878 teachers could have been written at any time in the last ten years and not come as a surprise:

> 86 per cent of full-time primary teachers feel they have insufficient time to do their job as it should be done.

> 70 per cent of full-time primary teachers think that the amount of time they spend doing their job in term time is unreasonable.

> 62 per cent of full-time primary teachers feel under uncomfortable pressure for more than half the time because of their workload.

> (p. 3)

So what is it that keep teachers in teaching? In this chapter we will explore this question with reference to teachers of all ages and experience, a consideration of work psychology and some reflections on how which factors can influence the often delicate balance between potential negative stress and motivation.

Starting out

Cockburn (2000) observed that (from a small sample) of teachers who acknowledged enjoying their work, most 'tend to aspire to being teachers for a considerable time prior to embarking on their training' (p. 231). Indeed, as Denholm (2001) suggests, some do so despite the odds,

> Mr Clark, who was one of only ten male students out of a class of 170 . . . said 'I always wanted to be a teacher and there was never any doubt in my mind that I wanted to work in the primary sector . . . but there is a problem with people not perceiving the job to be particularly macho.'
>
> (p. 5)

What creates such high motivation? On surveying 24 former PGCE primary students in their first year of teaching they all – without exception – said that they enjoyed the job because of the children. Typical comments from younger and older NQTs on enjoyable aspects of the job were:

> 'The hours in the classroom and seeing the children happy and progressing.'
>
> (F under 25 years)

> 'When children are pleased at understanding something or doing something that they thought they couldn't do.'
>
> (M 26–35 years)

> 'The excitement from seeing a child's work that is far better, in whatever aspect, than expected.'
>
> (F between 36–45 years)

> 'The buzz when a lesson goes really well.'
>
> (F over 45 years)

Two also included positive feedback from colleagues and parents,

> 'Positive comments from Head, Deputy or colleague.'
>
> (F between 36–45 years)

> 'Positive feedback from staff and parents.'
>
> (F between 36–45 years)

In passing, it may be interesting to note that these last two comments come from older NQTs.

In essence, it is likely that all these individuals were experiencing what Hackman and Oldham (1980) describe as internal motivation on the job as, according to their theory, the essential conditions were met:

1   The teachers had knowledge of the results of their work.
2   They experienced responsibility for the results.
3   They perceived their work as meaningful.

Indeed, Hackman and Oldham conclude, 'It appears necessary for all three of these factors . . . to be present for strong internal work motivation to develop and persist' (p. 73).

In contrast, Laura Mannering (a first-class graduate from Cambridge with a 'glowing' report from her teacher training college) explains that, as an NQT, 'by Christmas I hated the job, had failed at it and had resigned' (TES, 23 October 1998, p. 6). She concludes that, 'I feel that my fall from bees-knees to also-ran could have been avoided' (ibid: 6). It seems that part of Laura's problem was a lack of support, 'Although I had a mentor, we met only once during the first half-term' (ibid: 6).

A total of 80 per cent of those in our survey of 24 NQTs clearly appreciated the support offered by colleagues,

> 'a smile round the door in the morning to check you're okay for the day makes all the difference.'
>
> (F 36–45 years)

> 'I'm lucky to have people around to ask for advice without feeling stupid.'
>
> (F under 25 years)

Not all of them specifically mentioned mentors, but those who did had a clear view as to their role which included 'being there' and 'someone who is friendly but keeps a close eye and only tells you things when needed, for example, explains sports day in May ready for June rather than in September' (F under 25). Having concluded that 'supportive and friendly staff are CRUCIAL!', one person added, 'The role of mentor is important and often not conducted properly.' The recent revision of induction procedures may have given mentors and induction tutors a greater role but time will tell whether the changes are sufficient.

More generally, it is important that teachers feel comfortable working with their colleagues. Arnold *et al.* (1998) note,

> mistrust of fellow workers is connected with high role ambiguity, poor communications and psychological strain in the form of low job satisfaction and to feelings of job-related threat to one's well-being.
>
> (p. 435)

Further, Spear *et al.* (2000) warn that,

> If teachers feel undervalued and under-appreciated by the public, then social relationships among colleagues within the school environment become even more important.
>
> (p. 19)

Seventeen of the 24 NQTs also found that lack of time was a major problem for them. In essence they found themselves with far too much to do. In part, providing NQTs with some non-contact time will help relieve the situation, but it is also important to recognise the different frustrations lack of time creates so that each can be managed in an appropriate manner.

Understandably people new to a profession take longer to do things than their more experienced colleagues. In teaching, some of this relates to preparing sessions for the first time, but it takes time for people to find their way around – 'finding materials' – and to undertake tasks which are still relatively new to them: 'I spend a vast amount of time on display work but I am sure it must get easier with experience.' Providing a helpful mentor and some extra time should help relieve such time pressures to enable teachers to enter their second year better equipped.

There are, however, some other issues relating to time pressures which give cause for concern and require further consideration. The first relates to the perennial problem of paperwork. As will be discussed below, teachers of all ages and experience consider that there is just too much of it. We are sure most would recognise the need for accountability and monitoring of pupil progress but would argue that there is scope for greater creativity and innovation. Is there a need for a teacher to mark every piece of work? Clearly from the point of view of assessing pupil attainment and preparing work accordingly, there is a need for practitioners to monitor pupil progress but this might often be done more effectively during a session where a task can be adjusted in the light of a child's response. This, too, would have the benefit of immediate feedback to pupils and reduce the possibility of conceptual misunder-standings (see, for example, Bennett *et al.* 1984).

Further, despite this age of litigation and accountability, do all – or, more realistically, many – teachers' actions need to be recorded? Perhaps the approach of a headteacher in an earlier study by Cockburn (1996) is more realistic,

> Long ago I decided that the people who work here come first and, if I get time, I'll complete a form and if I don't get time then it doesn't get completed. If it's really urgent they'll send me another one. And if it's desperate they'll probably phone as well.
>
> (p. 99)

Now we are not suggesting that we add to the administrators' workload by expecting them to be constantly chasing everyone up but it is salutary to note that the above remark was followed up with the same head recalling,

> One summer, when I was sorting things out, I found all sorts of forms and I thought, 'Oh God, I should have sent that back' and 'Oh heck, that should have gone'. And then I suddenly realised no one had ever chased me, no one had ever asked me, so how important was it in the first place?
>
> (p. 99)

Time constraints can also contribute to two very serious pressures. The first relates to the personal lives of NQTs,

> Teaching has taken over every aspect of my life in term time at the expense of my family, friends, boyfriend (now ex) and any form of life I had before I started.
>
> (F 26–35 years)

The second pressure is a frustration that many remarked on when time constraints prevented them from doing the job as they would like,

> 'Not enough hours in the day to do everything properly.'
>
> (F 36–45 years)

> 'Not enough school hours to do the things you'd like and having to skim over subjects (especially in literacy) to fulfil the curriculum.'
>
> (F 36–45 years)

'Limited opportunity to do interesting work in a subject due to time constraint.'

(M 26–35 years)

'Not having enough time to be the teacher I really want to be.'

(F 26–35 years)

The net effect was for some, as one teacher remarked, that, 'There is a feeling that you cannot control your time and days and weeks blur into one' (F 36–45 years). Another explained that, for her, 'Any rewards/ motivations I had when I began teaching have slowly eroded to nothing' (F 26–35 years).

Moreover, as Laura Mannering, who was discussed earlier, mentioned in her article in *TES*,

> One mistake I made was that I never gave myself time to enjoy life . . . I returned to school after the October half-term holiday exhausted, as I had come into school for four of my five days off.
>
> (p. 6)

She went on to illustrate the consequences,

> As my tiredness increased, my enthusiasm and control over the class weakened . . . My errors of judgement over behaviour and time management, as well as fatigue, contributed to the crisis in my class.
>
> (ibid: 6)

In such situations a downward spiral can occur for, as one of the NQTs in our study said, 'Having no spare time can be exhausting and demoralising' (F 26–35 years).

Hackman and Oldham (1980) explain,

> When someone has high internal work motivation, feelings are closely tied to how well he or she performs on the job. Good performance is an occasion for self reward, which serves as an incentive for continuing to do well. And because poor performance prompts unhappy feelings, the person may elect to try harder in the future so as to avoid those unpleasant outcomes and regain the internal rewards that good performance can bring.
>
> (pp. 71–2)

Unfortunately, as described above, some NQTs find it increasingly difficult to overcome the difficulties induced by their inexperience and exhaustion. Somehow a way needs to be found for them to return to, 'a self-perpetuating cycle of positive work motivation powered by self-generated (rather than external) rewards for good work' (ibid: 72).

Hackman and Oldham (1980) continue,

> People who are *not* competent enough to perform well will experience a good deal of unhappiness and frustration at work, precisely because the job 'counts' for them and they do poorly at it.
>
> (ibid: 84)

The outcomes they explain,

> rather than continually accept the pain of failing that is experienced as important, such individuals frequently opt to withdraw from the job – either behaviourally, by changing jobs, or psychologically, by convincing themselves that in fact they do *not* care about the work.
>
> (ibid: 84)

Given that 36 or 38 weeks is a very short time in which to prepare someone for a highly demanding profession and, given that there is wide variation in the situations in which NQTs find themselves, it seems crucial that considerable external support and guidance are provided in the very early weeks of the induction year. Time and attention invested there to enhance NQTs' competencies and confidence would, in our view, be money very well spent and would reduce the likelihood of individuals leaving the profession. Some might argue that not many leave in the early months but, given their initial commitment and personal investment, it is important to recognise that the erosion of motivation and self-confidence can continue for several years before a teacher finally decides to quit the profession.

Carter and Francis (2001) also hold our view,

> The support provided to beginning teachers at this time is critical to the quality of their immediate professional experiences as well as to their longer-term professional learning.
>
> (p. 249)

Indeed they quote Veenman (1984), who argues that beginning a career in teaching resembles a process of transition or rite of passage along the lines of a 'reality shock'.

Apart from time constraints and issues of paperwork, a quarter of the teachers in our survey of NQTs mentioned behaviour management as a problem. One male NQT explained how frustrating it was when, 'a carefully-prepared lesson was ruined by bad behaviour by a few pupils' (M 26–35 years). Another said, 'It is the same couple of children who compete for attention and it's hard to relax and really enjoy the lesson when you're worried about what they'll do next' (F 25 years or under).

Closely related to this is the issue of differentiation, which clearly some also found difficult. The Teacher Training Agency (2002) reached similar conclusions after surveying more that 5,500 NQTs and reports that,

> The new standards for Qualified Teacher Status set out in Qualifying to Teach, which come into effect in September 2002, take account of the need for NQTs to be well prepared for the challenges they will meet in the classroom, including behaviour management, pupil diversity and the use of ICT. The new standards should help ensure that those who qualify in future will have benefited from training more closely focused on their needs.
>
> (p. 2)

In other words, on qualifying, teachers should be better prepared for classroom life than in the past.

In addition, 'Following many years of patchy and inconsistent induction practice' (Williams *et al.* 2001: 253) in England, serious attention is being given to the induction process. On taking up their first post, every NQT should be assigned an induction tutor. The role of the induction tutor in England is outlined in Figure 5.1 which comes with the following statement:

> You (the induction tutor) are not expected to be the sole provider of every aspect of an NQT's induction. Headteachers and governing bodies have the ultimate responsibility for making sure that each NQT is provided with an appropriate programme of monitoring, support and assessment.
>
> (TTA 2001: 4, brackets added)

Williams *et al.* (2001) go further to stress the importance of appropriate communities and cultures recognising that the atmosphere of a school can play an important role in supporting NQTs. They cite Henrietta, who had just started at a secondary school,

In developing and providing an effective induction programme, an induction tutor should work with the NQT to:

- recognise and develop the NQT's strengths
- build on the NQT's Career Entry Profile while recognising new or different development needs arising from the NQT's first teaching post
- encourage the NQT to contribute to and evaluate the induction programme
- make effective and well targeted use of the NQT's release time
- arrange focused classroom observations both of and by the NQT
- draw on expertise and resources, within and beyond the school, to arrange for professional development opportunities appropriate to the NQT's needs
- provide constructive feedback, and arrange for the NQT to meet, and discuss particular issues with other colleagues
- help the NQT to develop their self-evaluation skills
- make sure that records are kept and that evidence is collected towards the formal assessment of the NQT's progress.

Figure 5.1 The role of the induction tutor (TTA 2001: 4)

It's not just teaching staff but like the lady on reception, she's very supportive, she will come and chat with us informally, and you know it's great . . . the staff in this school have gone out of their way to sort of involve us and make us their friends.

(p. 263)

Given that NQTs have specific requirements, however, it is also important that they have regular meetings and structured support with their mentors which recognise and work on their *specific individual* needs. The skill required to do this should not be underestimated for, although, as discussed above, there are some issues many NQTs find difficult (for example, time management, paperwork), there is not a formula which can be applied to all. Rather, mentors need to use skills to appreciate the needs of their NQT in their particular situation and act accordingly. Carter and Francis (2001) warn against the possibility of,

Workplace learning restricted to simple hierarchical apprenticeship (which) serves only to replicate the past and reinforce the conservation and conformism that has characterised pedagogy in many schools.

(p. 260)

Although we very much welcome the formalised introduction of mentoring we wish to stress that its operationalisation needs to be carefully monitored: time and appropriate education must be given to mentors to ensure that they do not perpetrate the notion of quick fixes – such as prepared lesson plans – and risk the possibility of NQTs becoming, in effect, technicians who manage – rather than educate – children. Providing superficial tips to newcomers to the profession may keep them in the job a little longer than if they receive no assistance but, not only is it detrimental for their pupils, but it also makes it highly likely that the teachers will cease to appreciate the real challenges and rewards of teaching successfully. The net effect is possible boredom and a desire to leave the profession for a more interesting occupation. Certainly the profession needs highly skilled practitioners and – if Scottish NQTs are anything to go by – that is what new teachers wish to become,

> From the list of twenty-eight elements in the survey, four of the elements were each identified by over 90 per cent of the sample (420 NQTs) as being central to the concept of professionalism:
>
> 1   Being able to self-evaluate the quality of one's own teaching (94 per cent)
> 2   Being enthusiastic about teaching and in so doing encouraging pupils to become learners (91 per cent)
> 3   Having a commitment to career-long professional development (91 per cent)
> 4   Working in collaboration with other professionals, parents and members of the community (91 per cent)
>
> (Purden 2001: 112, brackets added)

The middle years

On the successful completion of their probationary period, teachers typically take on a full timetable and, within a relatively short space of time, may take on additional roles such as subject co-ordinator or year leader. It is also a time for consolidation of skills learnt and might be described as a 'transition period' (Fullan 1993). Explicit support – such as from a mentor – will have been reduced and, in many cases, removed. When such changes occur, it is particularly important to recognise that,

> motivation does not remain constant during the course of months or years. Rather, it is characterised by regular (re)appraisal and

balancing of the various internal and external influences to which the individual is exposed.

(Dörnyei 2001: 16)

As will be discussed later in the chapter, Dörnyei (2001) considers that there are four motivational aspects with respect to teacher motivation, but the one which may be particularly relevant during the transition period of decreasing support is the fragility of the emotions when exposed to several negative influences. Thus, if too much extra time and effort is required, anxiety and stress levels may be raised with a corresponding decrease in motivation.

On surveying 23 teachers in their third year of teaching, it was apparent that for the most part they still enjoyed teaching. Reasons for this included,

'The "wow" factor of learning.'

(F 25 or under)

'No two days are the same.'

(F 26–35 years)

'Sharing knowledge.'

(F 36–45 years)

Just over half of them found it very frustrating when they were asked to do things which they viewed as unnecessary or irrelevant.

'Endless meetings about very little.'

(F 26–35 years)

'Paperwork which I know I don't need and which I am sure that no one else ever reads.'

(F 25 years or under)

'Being overloaded with extra jobs, techniques, paperwork or activities that provide no benefit for pupils, usually requested at short notice, and often very time consuming.'

(F 26–35 years)

This, coupled with lack of time, was demoralising and, in some cases, might well tip the balance between staying on and leaving the profession.

It *may* be that some teachers do not fully appreciate the reasoning behind what is being asked of them. In which case, work needs to be done on ensuring that they recognise the importance and significance of, in particular, non-classroom-based activities. In our view the responsibility for this should lie with the perpetrator of the task(s), although it often appears that an intermediary is involved, particularly when it is a government-led initiative. This will be considered more fully below when the issue of change is discussed but here it is clear that headteachers and/or subject leaders could have a pivotal role, either as responsible initiators of tasks or reliable conveyors of requests who are satisfied with what is being demanded. The situation is not helped if such leadership is weak for, as one teacher said, 'Poor leadership causes a great deal of stress amongst staff' (F over 45 years).

On being established

One might imagine that if one is an established and successful teacher, then thoughts of leaving the profession after several years will be much reduced. That may be the case but, recalling Dörnyei's (2001) point that teacher motivation is fragile and susceptible to negative influences, it is important to consider possible factors which might disturb the balance between enjoying the job and contemplating leaving it.

With age and experience come a variety of benefits including, for many, enhanced self-esteem. Reviewing a range of studies on the subject, Andrews (1998) reports, 'All studies show positive shifts occurring in the middle years, particularly between ages 40 and 50' (p. 341). Coupled with that, teachers usually find themselves with increased responsibilities (see below) and just as much, if not more, to do. Sadly, for most of us, as we get older our stamina begins to wane and, for some teachers, exhaustion can begin to become a real problem. Several years ago a teacher used a Norfolk expression to describe how she felt, 'I could fall asleep on a washing line.' At the same time a significant minority find themselves with ageing relatives to consider, which can take time, energy and attention away from the job. Recent proposals at our university include a facility for taking time away from work to care for family members who have become dependent. It is as yet unclear as to the financial implications of such an idea but the suggestion is a good one and such awareness of the realities of life might well be extended to the teaching profession.

Since their introduction, the manner in which inspections have been conducted in England has changed in response to criticisms and pressures. They are now intended to be of a lighter touch and less warning is given to reduce the months of pressure which seem to build up after an inspection is announced. Part of the problem for older teachers is that they tend to be well established in their ways and they find change – for example, so that they can be seen to fulfil Ofsted requirements – difficult. Many also find it stressful to be observed and judged. Tina, a first school teacher with eight years' experience, described it thus,

> It really felt like a kind of violation that the inspectors came in, sat there, watched you teaching and took part of you away with them. And I felt like just chasing them down the corridor and saying, 'What did you think?'

Jeffrey and Woods (1998) report what Cloe said of the experience,

> I've had a lot of things to cope with and the old body's kept going and I haven't had too many worries about illnesses but I was so run down and low beforehand. I'm still not well and it's called into question what you're doing to yourself as a human being. You start thinking to yourself, 'Why are you going through this? What are you doing to yourself? Why are you doing this to yourself?'
>
> (p. 122)

We are not saying that we are against inspections and the need for accountability per se but simply that the effects need to be fully understood. It may still be the case that the perceived benefits in the form of higher standards may well be outweighed by the unseen short- and longer-term effects which may result in teachers leaving the profession. Talking more generally, Jade, an experienced teacher in her thirties, said that there is, 'a lack of recognition about the realities of working in a school'. She went on to expand on some of these,

> It's the time spent on counselling parents, dealing with disruptive children and parents keen on rights but not responsibilities and the masses of paperwork to name just a few!

In our view greater insight into teachers' working lives over a prolonged period is required to appreciate the job as it is for a wide range of people in a wide range of situations, how they perceive it and the effects of change as it applies to both their work and their emotions. Interestingly Briner (1999) observed,

It is . . . unfortunate and curious that in conceptualising and researching how people feel at work, psychologists have almost completely ignored emotion.

(p. 16)

Briner acknowledges that for methodological reasons such research would not be easy but, given that teachers are expected to be 'professional' at all times, it seems that further research is required. What, for example, is the effect of having to adopt a role when one is unwell, having a hard time at home or whatever? Does such masking take its toll such that it moves some to leave the profession? What, if anything, could be done to alter that? Some insight into a possible way forward comes from Csikszentmihalyi (1992), 'It is not the skills we actually have that determine how we feel, but the ones we think we have' (p. 75).

A final issue we need to consider, particularly in relation to more experienced teachers, is the concept of change. There have been a lot of changes in education throughout the UK in recent years and teachers we have spoken to have clearly found it a problem. When asked what were the most frustrating aspects of the job,

'The need to implement too much too soon.'

(F 26–35 years)

'The paper-pushing tasks and the constant changing ideas and policies which are forced on us from government.'

(F 26–35 years)

'Even more frustrating than the dictated policies are the facts that (1) they come so quickly without giving schools the opportunity to fully implement and be comfortable with the last policy; (2) the powers that be so frequently change their philosophy and thinking about education that quite fundamental changes are made to the way teaching is addressed.'

(F 36–45 years)

'Change after change in curriculum being foisted upon us by people who have no idea themselves how to implement it.'

(F 26–35 years)

Here we will not take issue with the changes per se but rather the fact that they have often been done without due regard for the complexities surrounding the process of change. The subject has been discussed extensively elsewhere – mostly notably by Fullan (1993, 1999) – but, in essence, there are five key points to recognise.

The first is that it is not by accident that classrooms operate in the way they do. As Greeno (1980) explained,

> The nature of the concepts and skills to be acquired [in school] has been shaped by a process of evolution in which materials that cannot be learned by most students and methods of instruction that are patently unsuccessful have been eliminated over the years.
>
> (p. 726)

Second, it often depends on where the move to change originates and whether those who have to implement it have a full understanding and appreciation as to what is required. Clearly the teachers above felt that changes were 'foisted upon' them. Perhaps understandable when one reflects on Sikes' (1992) suggestion that,

> motivating all (imposed) changes lies the assumption (which may or may not be justified) that all is not well and that students are not receiving the best education because teachers and their teaching is inappropriate or inadequate.
>
> (p. 37)

Imposed change also, in effect, reduces some of a teacher's autonomy, autonomy being an important facet of teacher motivation (Dörnyei 2001).

Third, it is important to recognise what can happen when changes are imposed. Kamii (1985) has a very apt description for this when teachers become 'mere executors (if not executioners) of someone else's decision' (p. xiv). Feiman-Nemser and Loden (1986) noted that teachers tend to be 'most receptive to proposals for change that fit in with current classroom procedures and . . . (do) not cause major disruptions' (p. 516). Having said that, if teachers do adopt changes as suggested, there is often a period of 'de-skilling' and a subsequent – albeit usually temporary – reduction in performance levels (MacDonald 1973). Other teachers become 'symbolic users' (Tabachnick 1981) thus, possibly not consciously, avoiding the effort of innovation and the accompanying drop in performance.

A fourth point to note is that, in attempts to ease the introduction of, for example, a way of working, some people produce material which may appear helpful but which is, in fact, detrimental. An example is to 'teacher-proof' material (Spodek and Rucinski 1984) so that teachers are instructed step by step as to what is required of them as they teach. We have serious concerns about teachers regurgitating someone else's plans without fully digesting them and adapting them to suit their particular needs and situations. Moreover, and particularly pertinent to this book, if teachers resort to such strategies, some of the challenges of really educating children will be removed. As discussed in Chapter 2, challenge is an important part of making teaching an attractive career.

Finally, one of the problems of frequent changes in education is that rarely is any innovation properly evaluated. Sometimes ideas are piloted but usually for an insufficient length of time. Then they are implemented and then – it sometimes feels like – they are superseded by another idea before anyone can properly assess whether they are effective or not.

The above is not to suggest that teachers are against change per se. Indeed, in an earlier study Cockburn (1996) quoted two teachers as saying,

> I used to find change difficult to cope with but I think I actually like change . . . I can't stand it if things stay the same.
>
> (p. 127)

> I believe that if you're not changing then you've had it really. You've become complacent and you're not moving on and you're not sort of reflecting on what you're doing.
>
> (p. 127)

In summary, change of any description is often more difficult than it might appear at first sight. Imposing it makes it considerably more complex and Fullan and Hargreaves (1992) caution that teacher developers must 'actively listen to and sponsor the teacher's voice' (p. 5). They also emphasise that, to be successful, older members of staff must be included in this as 'most approaches still fail to value (and consequently fail to involve) the veteran teacher' (p. 5). (You may note that this was written over ten years ago but, sadly, in our view, the same is true today.) To summarise at least one teacher's thoughts on change in another way,

> The Government should stop complaining about low standards and poor behaviour and children not reading. They do! . . . Let us

get on with our jobs and occasionally give us a pat on the back for what we do.

(Laura, in Cockburn 2000: 230)

Continuing professional development for experienced teachers

Recognising the complexities surrounding change in no way dismisses the importance of continuing professional development for experienced teachers,

> Though initial teacher education provides a sound basis for the teaching task, the dynamic nature of society, together with new ideas and thinking about the learning and teaching process, means that teacher education must be a continuous process throughout a teacher's career.
>
> (Livingston and Robertson 2001: 186)

Throughout the UK this is being recognised, however, it is still early days and there are still thorny issues to be addressed. For example, Mortimer and Mortimer (1989) noted that teachers most in need of INSET tend not to go on voluntary courses. Doing professional development properly takes time and energy: who is going to fund teachers' release time so that they are fresh and receptive and who will cover their classes in such times of teacher shortage? (see Chapter 6).

It is absolutely crucial that, if teachers' continuing professional development is to be managed successfully, it must be done with a clear understanding of:

• both teachers' personal and professional needs
• the contexts in which they work
• teaching and learning processes.

And teachers must, 'have the opportunity to have a central role in making decisions about their own professional development' (Livingston and Robertson 2001: 193).

Additionally, and most important of all, teachers must feel inspired and challenged by these ventures so that not only are they motivated to stay in the profession but that they also return to their classrooms ready to educate their pupils in as effective and successful a manner as possible.

Note

1   The authors would like to thank the Town Close Charity for their financial contribution which funded the survey discussed in this chapter.

References

Andrews, B. (1998) 'Self-esteem', *The Psychologist*, 11: 339–42.

Arnold, J., Cooper, C.L. and Robertson, I.T. (1998) *Work Psychology: Understanding Human Behaviour in the Workplace*, London: Financial Times/Pitman Publishing.

Association of Teachers and Lecturers (1998) Summary of Findings of the First Report, London: Association of Teachers and Lecturers.

Bennett, N., Desforges, C., Cockburn, A. and Wilkinson, B. (1984) *The Quality of Pupil Learning Experiences*, London: Lawrence Erlbaum Associates.

Briner, R. (1999) 'Feeling and Smiling', *The Psychologist*, 12: 16–19.

Carter, M. and Francis, R. (2001) 'Mentoring and beginning teachers' workplace learning', *Asia-Pacific Journal of Teacher Education*, 29: 249–62.

Cockburn, A.D. (1996) *Teaching under Pressure*, London: Falmer Press.

Cockburn, A.D. (2000) 'Elementary teachers' needs: issues of retention and recruitment', *Teaching and Teacher Education*, 16: 223–38.

Csikszentmihalyi, M. (1992) *Flow: The Psychology of Happiness*, London: Rider.

Denholm, A. (2001) 'Wanted: men to become primary teachers', *The Scotsman*, 2 October.

Dörnyei, Z. (2001) *Teaching and Researching Motivation*, Harlow, UK: Longman.

Evans, L. (1998) *Teacher Morale, Job Satisfaction and Motivation*, London: Paul Chapman Publishing.

Feiman-Nemser, S. and Loder, R.E. (1986) 'The cultures of teaching', in M.C. Wittrock (ed.), *Handbook of Research in Teaching* (3rd edition), New York: Macmillan.

Fullan, M. (1993) *Change Forces*, London: Falmer Press.

Fullan, M. (1999) *Change Forces: The Sequel*, London: Falmer Press.

Fullan, M. and Hargreaves, A. (1992) 'Teacher development and educational change', in M. Fullan and A. Hargreaves (eds), *Teacher Development and Educational Change*, London: Falmer Press.

Greeno, J.C. (1980) 'Psychology of learning 1960–1980: one participant's observations', *American Psychologist*, 35: 713–28.

Hackman, J.R. and Oldham, G.R. (1980) *Work Redesign*, Reading, MA: Addison-Wesley.

Jeffrey, B. and Woods, P. (1998) *Testing Teachers*, London: Falmer Press.

Kamii, C. (1985) *Young Children Reinvent Arithmetic*, New York: Teachers' College Press.

Livingston, K. and Robertson, J. (2001) 'The coherent system and the empowered individual: continuing professional development for teachers in Scotland', *European Journal of Teacher Education*, 24: 183–94.

MacDonald, B. (1973) 'Innovation and incompetence', in D. Harningser (ed.), *Towards Judgement: The Publications of the Evaluation Unit of the Humanities Curriculum Project 1970–72*, occasional Paper 1, Centre for Applied Research in Education, University of East Anglia.

Mortimer, P. and Mortimer, J. (1989) 'School focus on inservice education, England and Wales', *Journal of Education for Teachers*, 15: 133–9.

Purden, A. (2001) 'New teachers' perspectives on continuing professional development', *Scottish Educational Review*, 33: 110–22.

Sikes, P.J. (1992) 'Imposed change and the experienced teacher', in M. Fullan and A. Hargreaves (eds), *Teacher Development and Educational Change*, London: Falmer Press.

Smithers, A. and Robinson, P. (2000) *Attracting Teachers: Past Patterns, Present Policies, Future Prospects*, Liverpool: Carmichael Press.

Spear, M., Gould, K. and Lee, B. (2000) 'Who would be a teacher?', project report produced on behalf of the National Foundation for Educational Research, Slough.

Spodek, B. and Rucinski, E.A. (1984) 'A study of early childhood teachers' beliefs', paper presented at the Annual Meeting of the American Educational Research Association, New Orleans, April.

Tabachnick, B.R. (1981) 'Teacher education as a set of dynamic social events', in B.R. Tabachnick, T. Popkewitz and B.B. Szekely (eds), *Studying Teaching and Learning: Trends in Soviet and American Research*, New York: Praeger.

Teacher Training Agency (2001) *The Role of Induction Tutor: Principles and Guidance*, London: Teacher Training Agency.

Teacher Training Agency (2002) 'The Newly Qualified Teacher Survey 2002'. Online: http://www.canteach.gov.uk/nqt_survey.

Williams, A., Prestage, S. and Bedward, J. (2001) 'Individualism to collaboration: the significance of teacher culture to the induction of newly qualified teachers', *Journal of Education for Teaching*, 27: 253–67.

Chapter 6

How do schools attract and retain good supply teachers?

'Substitute teachers have remained largely absent from educational agendas' (Morrison 1999). Mention the term 'supply teacher' to any head or deputy headteacher and, almost inevitably, you will induce a response along the line of 'I had to phone fifty times this morning until I found someone available to come in today' or 'we have half a dozen excellent supply teachers we like to use but, unless we book them well in advance, it is almost impossible to get hold of them'.

There is no doubt about it that supply – or substitute – teachers are, quite literally, in very short supply in this country. Ironically, the situation is compounded by one of the strategies being used to retain good teachers and encourage returners, namely continuing professional development. If practitioners are to keep up to date, be enthused and stimulated – the argument goes – they are more likely to be confident, highly motivated and enthusiastic teachers. Continuing professional development takes time however and, if it is to be optimally effective, it is best done during the day when most teachers are freshest and most receptive. Providing teachers time away from the classroom also raises the status of such activities, adding to the notion that INSET, etc is an important part of professional life, rather than something incidental and unimportant which can be squeezed in at the end of a busy day. Clearly some professional development can be done as an entire staff when the school is closed to its pupils. Other professional development, however, is better done if tailored to the more individual needs of groups of teachers, be they new to the profession or more experienced, but in need of specific training. In both cases the course dates are generally known well in advance, giving more time to undertake the search for a suitable supply teacher. Covering the class of one newly qualified primary teacher under such circumstances is not generally a major problem. Trying to cover for ten – let alone twenty or thirty –

experienced secondary mathematics teachers within a county is considerably more of a problem. The situation is not helped when one encounters the following which, believe it or not, is a true story recounted to me first hand. Nigel, a highly experienced teacher, phoned up his local education authority (LEA) to ask to go on the supply register. He was told that he would need to complete a CRB (Criminals Record Bureau) form to ensure that he had not been convicted for any child-related offences before he could be taken on and that they would pop a form in the post for him to complete. Ten days later and no sign of the form, Nigel phoned the LEA again: they had forgotten him but, having confirmed his address, promised that they would send a form straight away. Another week goes by and still no form. Another phone call, lots of apologies and promises but nothing transpired, so Nigel abandoned the notion and spends his life pottering round the house instead while his wife continues to be the breadwinner.

One would hope that such tales are far from typical. But for them to happen at all is seriously disturbing. Who is to say what the effect of telling such an experience to others might have on teachers contemplating taking up supply work. If, therefore, you are someone involved in maintaining a supply list for your region, please take note and ensure that the process is rigorous – certainly – but as easy and straightforward as possible right from the first – often tentative – approach.

In this chapter we consider the working lives of supply teachers, exploring factors which attract and retain them in the role. It is based on the research literature, chance encounters and in-depth discussions with six teachers from across the age sector who have made a conscious decision to be professional supply teachers.

Problems

As discussed, putting your name on a supply list is not as easy as it might first appear. Indeed, the difficulties he faced put Nigel off altogether. In this section we explore some of the other potential problems supply teachers face and discuss how these might be avoided or, at least, minimised.

Before embarking on supply work it is important to recognise that, although there may be implicit assumptions regarding the obligations between teacher and school, no contracts will change hands between these parties (Dougherty 1998). The supply teacher may have a contract with an agency or county hall but the absence of one with the school may lead to misunderstandings when it comes to expectations. By law supply teachers are covered under the Health and Safety at Work Act (Dougherty 1998) but what about the extent and nature of their work? There is no legal requirement that supply teachers' work be clearly specified, resulting in a wide range of practices. Such variation in itself can be a problem, as it requires a high degree of flexibility on the part of supply teachers (see next section). Moreover, occasionally a supply teacher may feel that a school has gone too far in its interpretation of what is appropriate. If a supply teacher is a member of a union and wishes to complain, then they are entitled to do so. This, however, is not necessarily straightforward. It can be done through the union repre-sentative of any school they work in – the representatives represent the union rather than the school – or, failing that, it can be done through regional representatives (Dougherty 1998) – neither is particularly easy if one feels like a mistreated outsider. In other words, yet another reason for not becoming a supply teacher. Having said that, in times when there is a distinct lack of supply teachers, it is certainly not in a school's best interests to upset them: no obligations works both ways. There is also the added potential for supply teachers to talk down a school to others who might otherwise contemplate working there.

Two other points to consider before becoming a supply teacher. The first is whether you have the necessary skills: as discussed below it would be wrong to assume because you have had a successful teaching career, you will make a successful supply teacher.

Second, there is no promotion for supply teachers and career devel-opment opportunities are likely to be limited. One of our local schools asks their regular supply teachers to join them for INSET days as a matter of course but this is rare. Some people do not seek promotion; others use supply work to gain experience explicitly for promotion or a permanent post but, by and large, it is best to assume that long-term supply teaching is not a sensible career move for the ambitious.

For many teachers the need to bring in a supply teacher is usually seen in rather negative terms; for example, if someone is ill or a class needs covering while someone goes off to an in-service course. Indeed Morrison (1994) observed that 'Frequently, their entrance occurred during periods when the temporal equilibrium of school organisation was disturbed, sometimes acutely so' (p. 57). Couple that with the view that some teachers cannot understand why people should want to do supply work – 'I wouldn't do it for any money' (Morrison 1994: 48) – and you start to appreciate the problems before the supply teacher has even reached the classroom door!

Teachers' and pupils' views of a supply teacher tend to be strongly influenced by what has gone on before. If, for example, teachers are used to seeing supply teachers coming in, doing the minimum with the result that the children do little work and become unruly, then they are unlikely to welcome new supplies with open arms. In contrast, some children welcome new supplies for the very reason that experience suggests that little work will be required! Neither is likely to be an attractive prospect for potential supply teachers. A retired teacher now on the supply list, Hilda remarks,

> Some schools positively embrace you and the staff support you, and the children are discouraged from treating you badly . . . They make supply teachers a priority because they realise they depend on them so much nowadays. Other schools, you know, aren't as good, to be honest. Some are very bad with supply teachers: they have a very bad attitude towards them.

Judy, a bright and bubbly supply teacher in her late thirties, recalls,

> I was quite shocked with people . . . You can go into a staffroom and nobody will speak to you.

And Ingrid, a 40-year-old Early Years supply teacher reported that 'it took nearly a term before people would say "hello" to me or talk to me in the staff room'. Robin points out how stressful it can be 'going somewhere new and meeting people who are not being very co-operative'.

Supply teachers providing pupils with inappropriate work can arise from a number of reasons. Some are lack of experience and/or a lack of knowledge of the class. Others, however, are due to the notes left by the teacher. Judy explains,

> I've been to schools where the planning is so detailed it would take you a day to wade through it. And I've been to places where it's one line on a bit of paper and there's no way you get anything out of that!

Hilda recalled going into a class and finding,

> The work he'd left was completely inappropriate. It was not good enough and not relevant. Nor was it user-friendly. So I ended up having to do a lot of making up my own things for them to do.

She goes on to explain how the problem is exacerbated as,

> You never ever meet the person you are covering for. You can never sit and chat with them about how they want you to do their lessons.

The struggle for supply teachers to produce appropriately interesting work cannot be helped in cases where 'creativity remains partly hidden . . . because the outcomes of the supply work are ignored when the usual teacher returns' (Morrison 1994: 62).

As will be discussed below, providing suitable work and managing pupils becomes easier if you work with the same class over an extended period. As Linda describes, however, when an absence is unexpected or intermittent this is not always possible:

> I do think that sometimes it must disrupt the pupils if they have more than one supply person because a teacher is ill, struggles back too soon and then takes more time off. I think that's unsettling for the school and the pupils and I think they must sometimes resent that. Yet again their member of staff isn't in. Sometimes I think 'I'm glad I was in the first day and not towards the end of someone's illness' because I think it must be difficult for pupils.

The younger the children, the more difficult it can be, as Hilda explains that, for many young children their teacher 'is really like their surrogate mum . . . I think they find it very difficult when their teacher is away'.

Morrison (1994) suggests that headteachers' expectations of supply teachers tend to be pragmatic: 'Although there are exceptions . . . what the headteacher wants (from the supply teacher) is that there's no hassle . . . he or she doesn't want to know you're there' (p. 50).

The six supply teachers interviewed all expected the children to test them out – 'They try all the tricks in the book' (Hilda) – and, as will be discussed below, they all become proficient at dealing with such challenges. Judy, however, pointed out that sometimes there could be problems:

> You've no background behind things and I think I find that quite hard not knowing the background of the children. So you might have a child and their behaviour is really awful but you don't know why. Perhaps there is something you are doing or, you know, in a class situation it might be something that has happened before. I find that incredibly hard not knowing enough about them.

Neil simply said 'It is much more of an uphill struggle getting that relationship with the children.'

There are strategies for supply teachers to change these attitudes on an individual basis – such as smiling, showing willing and so on – but this book is more about recruiting and retaining them, so what can the schools do? This will be discussed further below but it is worth noting that it is not a straightforward issue as each situation is unique. Dougherty (1998) goes so far as to say, 'The temporary teacher's status depends upon so many variables that it changes from minute to minute' (p. 68).

The problems and ambiguities supply teachers face do not end beyond the classroom door: 'It is easy for a locum simply to be used: loaded with unpleasant, unfamiliar and extra tasks and sent off to have a miserable day' (Dougherty 1998: 72). Ingrid, for example, says 'and you nearly always have to do playground duty', while Hilda observes that recently 'in a lot of the primary schools they expect you to mark all the work you've done all day . . . I was really expected to do that and if I didn't sit there marking until 6 o'clock at night I was scorned by some of the other teachers and the headteacher'.

All six of the supply teachers interviewed said that they particularly like it when they had been in a school long enough to get to know the children. Morrison (1994) points out, however, that it can be 'a little bit tricky' (p. 55) when it is clear that someone will be absent for an extended period but no one is sure for how long. She interviewed one teacher about this who explained: 'I would not wish to try and totally re-organise a classroom situation. So I would feel under a degree of constraint not to necessarily organise things in the way you would wish to . . . it's a bit of a balancing act really' (p. 55).

Recently the number of requests for half-day supply cover has increased significantly because of the rise in half-day INSET courses. Neil says he finds this difficult as,

> You can't get booked for the second half of the day . . . There is no way you can get another school to book you, so effectively you're losing half a day's pay. Last year I counted up, I had 20 half days, so effectively that's two weeks' full money that you're missing out on.

LEAs' involvement in supply will be discussed in more detail below but, while on the issue of problems, Ingrid and Hilda both had complaints about their respective LEAs: 'I've had a one-day-a-week contract and I was doing the job for eight weeks before the contract came through' and 'You always have to wait for two or three months for your money when you work for the LEA.'

Necessary skills

Dougherty (1998) suggests that, in some ways, supply teachers have more in common with student teachers than their fully qualified colleagues. To make a success of their time in a school, both students and supply teachers need to recognise that they are visitors; they cannot make any lasting changes to the classroom; they are well-advised to fit in with someone else's regimes; and they need to be able to improvise quickly and effectively if they are unsure what to do. As Robert explains: 'It's important to be able to think on your feet, fit in, be flexible, be good at coping with new situations and getting on with people.'

As soon as they walk into a class for the first time a good supply teacher can size up the situation and adopt the appropriate entry style. Some people – such as Robert – find it exhilarating: 'I enjoy the bit of adrenalin rush you get from being somewhere new.' Full-time experienced teachers rarely think of how they will enter a room but it is something supply teachers need to perfect for every new situation. This is all part of being flexible: 'If a supply teacher is not flexible enough to cope with the changing demands of different schools then he/she is in the wrong job' (Dougherty 1998: 68). As Ingrid points out: 'Although you have more control when you work, what you don't have is control of what is actually going on when you go in there but, because you are only in there occasionally, you have to step back from that and not worry about it really and think "Well, this isn't how I would do it but never mind." You have to be flexible and fit in and try to do things in the way that their teacher does, even if that doesn't come naturally.'

It is also part of being sensitive to each situation and adapting what Good and Brophy (1987) term 'withitness'. This is something all effective teachers do all the time but it is just that much harder if one is unfamiliar with the children and the routines of the school. Hilda finds that, although each school is 'roughly the same . . . it's different on the minute details which you need to know'. There are strategies supply teachers can use to help with these difficulties, such as labelling, which, as Ingrid says, is better than shouting out 'oi you, you in the blue, look this way!' Neil adopts a higher order skill: 'The first thing that I normally do when I go into a class is share a lot of my personal information with the children so that I'm not just some other adult coming in and teaching them – I want them to have a bit more about me and I want them to give me their information about themselves . . . we've got a bit more of a bond.'

Robert also feels that he sometimes has to take risks which, if he were a permanent member of a school staff, would not be so calculated. He was not talking about responding to the 'oh not you again' comment from a child which, although tiresome, was easily dealt with. Rather, he was referring to situations where the children had not been well managed by their regular teacher:

> I've had children who aren't used to doing as they are asked and they almost literally climb up the walls and they suddenly realise there is someone whose will is not going to bend . . . There was a girl and (I knew) she was setting things up to make life difficult for me. I know she moved some furniture around and wouldn't move it back and she wouldn't do as she was told . . . She didn't have her shoes on and so I just removed them to another classroom . . . I was a bit worried as it was home time and the mum was outside so I went outside and explained and the mum was totally supportive!

So, within the classroom situation successful supply teachers need to demonstrate high degrees of sensitivity, flexibility and withitness because the situation is new and available information is usually limited. Dougherty (1998) also suggests that skills beyond the classroom can also be valuable: 'The supply teacher who is bright, friendly and pleasant is likely to attract favourable attention. This leads directly to more requests to do that or that, but has the advantage that the locum tends to be referred to by name' (p. 71). Reading this for the first time I was shocked: surely calling someone by name is basic good manners? Are supply teachers such non-people that *they* need to go out of their way to be addressed by their own name? Dougherty (1998) goes on to suggest that a friendly supply teacher might also become included in the coffee club and even come to be regarded as 'a real human being' who could 'be considered important' (p. 71). Again, these comments are a sad reflection on our staffrooms. So, added to the classroom skills, an effective supply teacher seemingly needs to be friendly and never out of sorts when they are in school. If, however, they appear to be a 'dull, grey figure who slumps in the corner of the staffroom, never speaking to anyone except to complain', they run the risk of being 'irrelevant' and 'even staff who would never consider being rude to someone they know by name may not worry too much about offending "the supply"' (Dougherty 1998: 71).

Given the problems faced and skills required, why does anyone even consider supply teaching?

Who are they and why do they do it?

Barlin and Hallgarten (2002) cite the DfEE (2001) who state that there were 19,000 occasional teachers in England in 2001 as compared to 12,200 in 1995. The former represent a little less than 4.5 per cent of the full-time equivalent workforce of teachers and the number is rising. Who are these people and are they supply teachers simply waiting for something better to come along?

A fairly common attitude towards supply teachers is to question why do they do it: if they are any good as teachers, then why do they not get a proper job? There are a range of people who undertake supply work. Some do it for very short periods, others for much longer, be it to fit in with their domestic situations or, simply, because they prefer it to finding themselves in the same situation day in, day out, teaching the same children.

Robert took up supply teaching after a very mediocre final teaching practice which made him wary:

> It is very difficult to tell sometimes what it is like to be in a school . . . until you are there . . . so I suppose a bit of me is a bit nervous about committing myself to something that might be horrendous . . . I did go and get a temporary job in Nottingham because we were thinking of moving and I did that for a term. That was a case in point . . . it was a nightmare . . . the Head was rather a large woman and she had these small hands . . . and she was a bully.

Many people take up supply teaching for the flexibility it affords as it fits in well with family commitments (Barlin and Hallgarten 2002). Typically, these are mothers such as 'Jane, for example, [who] aimed to return to full-time teaching "within four to five years" and [who] considered her current work enabled her to "keep in touch"' (Morrison 1994: 54). Similarly Robert does it as 'It is really flexible and you can go in early . . . pick your children up earlier . . . and you've got control over when you work.' Dougherty (1998) warns, however, that such flexibility can come with a price: should a supply teacher take a full week's work now, for example, or opt for three days a week for a longer period?

A definite benefit of such casual work for Robert is that 'although the children [in school] can be very irritating and stressful, you have more emotional energy, more patience and you can use your sense of humour with your own family more than when you are dragged down by it all in a permanent job'. Neil agrees, adding: 'I like the fact that I can go into school, have a really nice day and then leave and not have anything to do at home because I've got a young family and I just don't have the energy really.' Ingrid was even more emphatic: 'I think full-time teaching takes over your whole life and my partner teaches and so it's bad enough there is one parent stressed out and during the term he hasn't got time for anything else and I don't think our family could withstand two of us in permanent teaching posts. You know, there needs to be somebody who is there for the children.'

Another very important factor for Robert was that it was 'money, easy money, better money in terms of what I could get elsewhere'. He did, however, find it tiresome that frequently 'you don't get paid for nearly seven weeks'.

Some parents use supply teaching as a way back into work to test the water and to regain their confidence after an extended period away (Morrison 1994). Ingrid explained: 'I think you lose confidence when you've been out for a while and I was thinking "oh no, I don't want to teach", but when I got back in I thought "oh actually I do really enjoy this"'. As implied above, however, such individuals need to select where they work very carefully to avoid being put off the profession altogether. Given the focus of this book is primarily on recruiting and retaining full-time teachers, Judy's description of how she became – and stayed – being a supply teacher is illuminating:

> 'Well, I'd been in the same school for ten years and I felt I needed a break and go to a different school. I wasn't quite sure of jumping from one to the next. And I thought that supply teaching is a good way to get out, go into a lot of schools and broaden my horizons . . . But I have to say that I have enjoyed supply work more than I thought I would and I just don't see me going back into a full-time job because I don't think it is worth it. I think there are too many stress factors.'

Moving to a new area can also be a catalyst to take up supply work. In part it may be because an area is difficult to break into when one is unknown. Our newly qualified teachers, for example, find it much easier to find posts in Norfolk than in other counties where they and our course are not so well known. In part, people opt for supply in such situations to find their way around an area and to explore the options open to them.

Morrison (1994) reports on Russ, who was broadening his horizons for another reason by taking up supply work:

> I wanted a bit of time to do what I enjoy doing, which is teaching children . . . It's given me a lot of opportunity to evaluate the strengths and weaknesses of the way management works in different schools . . . whether I choose to return to educational management or whether I will be looking at some specialist off-shoot, that's really something to be decided over the next couple of years.
>
> (p. 54)

In passing, I suspect few potential managers take up the opportunity to see other schools in action by way of supply work but perhaps they should to prepare them for their future roles, for Robert suggests: 'I know schools better – apart from the people who work there – than Ofsted inspections, parents and anybody else. So supply teachers are a good resource. They know exactly what is going on in schools. There is a lot of knowledge there that could be used.' Sadly, such knowledge can sometimes be passed on and the supply teacher suffers as a consequence: over a period of several days Hilda noticed that one of her pupils was fine before break but became aggressive and uninhibited after it. She reported to the deputy head that she suspected the girl of taking drugs. The reply was: 'Oh we don't have drugs in our school' and she was never asked back. Later she happened to be discussing the matter with a policeman friend and his response was: 'It's very difficult in that school because nobody acknowledges the problem.' As a result, Hilda is more cautious in what she says: 'You don't tend to rock the boat too much if you are a supply teacher.'

The retired also take on a significant role when it comes to supply work as schools will frequently call upon retired colleagues to cover classes. A major advantage is that little induction is required although, with the rapidity of educational innovations, there is a possibility of the supply teacher being a little out of date. Hilda found it hard to give up work completely on her retirement: 'I wanted the flexibility that supply teaching gives you.' After several long-term jobs she was asked to do supply in an area where the children are known to be 'very, very difficult'. She explained:

This young lady had left the school with a nervous breakdown. I did the odd day and it seemed quite a reasonable school. I quite liked it and they said 'Can you come in and do from February half-term right through to the end of the summer?' and I said 'Well look, I'll come on a supply basis and see how it goes.' Thank goodness I didn't sign a contract or anything. After a week I just couldn't cope with it. It was the nature of the children. They were either disturbed or badly behaved. I could understand why her health failed.

There is also an increasing number of supply teachers from overseas (Barlin and Hallgarten 2002). Sometimes it is part of their world travels and sometimes it is in response to our need for teachers.

One of Morrison's (1994) interviewees also explained that, for some 'the gypsy gets into them . . . some people actually like the uncertainty of getting up in the morning and not knowing what class they'll have till they get there' (p. 47). Linda explains that she likes the 'variety and challenge: no two days are ever the same'. Judy points out that an added bonus is that, 'if there was something that was really bad then you'd never have to go back there. It's nice knowing you've got an option!'

Apart from the flexibility and frisson provided by supply teaching, are there any other aspects of the work that people seek? Morrison's (1994) interviewees 'spoke with an enthusiasm which was most marked when opportunities to spark children's interest depended on a skilful blending of expertise, experience and independence' (p. 56). Later she explains: 'Paradoxically, supply work enables some participants to concentrate on what they consider to be the core of teaching, namely the daily interactions between teacher and children in classroom settings, freed from the bureaucratic constraints of school organisations' (pp. 62, 63). Secondary supply teacher Hilda explains:

I love teaching history. It's lovely to be able to go into a class and actually sit down with them and talk to them and get involved with them . . . I also love teaching art and I'll go in and have a lovely time . . . I do love the kids. It keeps you young – I'm sure it does. And my husband likes me to do it because he says he can see a change in me. When I'm doing a bit of supply teaching he says I come home happy and I feel as though I'm doing (a) something useful, (b) I'm earning a bit of money and (c) I'm doing something I like doing and I'm with young people.

To summarise why all six interviewees continued being supply teachers: they clearly enjoyed it and, in essence, it contrasted very favourably with full-time teaching as it gave them back their life:

> When I was teaching full time I felt like I didn't have much sort of a private life. I was just too exhausted to enjoy life and I'd get to the holidays and – like all other teachers – I just sort of crashed . . . Teaching shouldn't take over your life like that.

Recommendations for recruiting and retaining high-quality supply teachers

One of the intentions of this chapter is to raise readers' awareness of supply teachers, their skills and the many potential difficulties they face. One of their greatest problems is their invisibility on the professional scene. Certainly, they achieve a high profile at 7.30 am when a deputy is desperately trying to get supply cover but, all too often, they are the forgotten teachers. Indeed, an A4 flyer issued by the General Teaching Council (GTC) specifying their priorities for 2001/2002 failed to mention supply teachers. Moreover, as mentioned earlier, they are entitled to be represented by a union representative in any school they have worked with for a minimum of half a day but how many union reps – let alone supply teachers – are aware of this? The first recommendation, therefore, is that all interested parties – the government, GTC, unions, LEAs, schools and supply teachers themselves – help to put supply teachers on the agenda and raise the professional profile.

Another related suggestion is to develop ways in which supply teachers can get to know one another and develop networks to reduce the sense of isolation experienced by many. Mullett (1994) set up a group of five supply teachers who first met as they picked up their own children in the primary school playground. They decided to meet as a 'Supply Teachers' Support Group', which clearly resulted in several benefits:

> Over the next few weeks we shared thoughts about useful books, games and activities for 'one off' days of supply work when the schools asked us to bring in suitable work. But often the part of the evening we enjoyed and valued most was to talk through the experience of teaching itself.
>
> (p. 32)

Rather than leaving such gatherings to chance it would seem sensible if all LEAs (some already do) more actively encouraged supply teachers to form such groups. Of course, in doing so, they run the risk of members of the groups sharing information on which schools are best avoided!

Having said that, it is clear that there are several steps that schools can easily take which would help encourage supply teachers to work there. Dougherty (1998) suggests that the task is up to the supply teacher:

> Teachers are competent professionals and the school management team are all teachers themselves. They will not have forgotten the problems which may affect the classroom teacher, but they might need a gentle reminder of the sort of support that is needed. The supply teacher can help him or herself out by simply behaving as if he or she is part of the school team: asking about potentially difficult circumstances before they occur, requesting support where it is needed and pointing out causes of dissatisfaction before they become major problems.
>
> (p. 65)

Certainly for the experienced supply teacher there is nothing intrinsically wrong with these suggestions but, both for pragmatic and professional reasons, we would argue that schools should take a more proactive role in welcoming and supporting supply teachers. Our interviewees had much to say on the subject and Hilda was particularly vocal:

> the Head of History had had a nervous breakdown and they (the school) were *very* accommodating: they paid my travel; they'd allow me to go in late if I wasn't teaching until a bit later in the morning and they didn't make me do any of the pastoral duties, like registering a form or going to assembly or any of that kind of thing.

She went on to explain that other schools she avoided – even though they were closer to home – as, for example:

> you trudge across to some grotty old mobile on the far side of the field and you come across an awful group of kids that nobody wants and they try to give you hell . . . some schools don't have a system – you don't know what to do – when you have a child who is an absolute pain. Other schools try. I've had very fraught-looking ladies

coming up to me and saying, 'Oh, I'm Head of Year for so-and-so. If you have any problems with him or her, just let me know or send them to me. I'm in room so-and-so.' I mean you hesitate to do it but at least you have something.

Carol summarised the thoughts of many,

> There is no shortage of offers of work in this area; I can pick and choose to work in the schools which I enjoy working in. Not all schools have cottoned on to this in the way that they treat supply teachers. Supply work can be very enjoyable and not too exhausting if you do it at places where you get well looked after.

Insider information and support can be invaluable and may depend on the classes involved. There is other information however, which schools can prepare and have readily available for any supply teachers. For example, Barlin and Hallgarten (2002) report that the Value For Money Unit recently suggested that schools provide induction material for supply teachers 'in the hope of engendering an atmosphere of support and encouragement' (p. 78). Such packs do not need to be long – indeed supply teachers would not have time to read them if they were – but they might include details of the routines of the day (e.g. lunchtime, home time), information about the class(es) and the school's policies for managing (mis)behaviour. All such information would help ensure a teacher's 'withitness' as discussed above.

A lack of structured continuing professional development is also a perceived problem for supply teachers. There are some distance learning packages available (DfEE 2000) but, given that isolation is also an issue, it would seem that locally organised courses for supply teachers would be more appropriate. If these were subsidised by LEAs, this might encourage participation and help raise supply teachers' – and others' – perception of their status. It might also help teachers see supply work as a valued career option rather than a stop gap. Barlin and Hallgarten (2002) report that 'many view themselves as freelance teachers', a term which, in our view, might also signal greater status to some than supply teacher.

In our view the issue of agency versus LEA supply lists should also be clarified. In many respects an agency has much to offer. For a school, agencies require one – not multiple – call(s) in the morning; they have a large number of teachers on their books and there is some quality assurance (Dougherty 1998). A supply teacher with an agency might also be in a stronger position than one on an LEA list in some cases where there is a disagreement between a school and the teacher. If the situation is serious enough, the agency might withdraw its services from the school whereas an LEA could not (Dougherty 1998).

To summarise, at times of teacher shortage, supply teachers are in the driving seat. If you need them, then you need to ensure that they are treated appropriately, otherwise they simply will not return. As discussed above and summarised by Carl below, not much extra effort is required by a school to make the difference,

> Some surprises . . . School C . . . small, not particularly challenging in terms of pupil behaviour. But just very pleasant . . . just left to get on with it, no induction, no welcome, left to your own devices. One school, difficult to get full complement of staff, not the easiest in terms of pupil behaviour . . . talk of having to go on to a 4-day week, but it was great, the staff there were very supportive, you felt part of the team. Really enjoyed it. Some local schools which I thought would be OK but turned out not to be, it's really very variable how supply teachers get treated . . . what happens when you first go into a school.

To conclude, however, as Thomas Day (1748–89) wrote,

> He [she] who undertakes the education of a child undertakes the most important duty of society. (Brackets added.)

If we seriously believe that, then surely all teachers – be they supply or not – should be treated as both people and professionals? Sadly our research has suggested that this is not always the case.

References

Barlin, D. and Hallgarten, J. (2002) 'Supply teachers: symptom of the problem or part of the solution?', in M. Johnson and J. Hallgarten (eds), *From Victims of Change to Agents of Change*, London: Institute of Public Policy Research.

DfEE (2000) *Supply Teachers: Meeting the Challenge*, London: DfEE.

Dougherty, M. (1998) *The Art of Surviving in Supply Teaching*, London: David Fulton Publishers.

General Teaching Council GTC *Priorities for 2001/02*. Occasional Flyer.

Good, T. and Brophy, J. (1987) *Looking in Classrooms*, New York: Harper and Row Publishers.

Morrison, M. (1994) 'Temps in the classroom: a case of hidden identities?', in S. Galloway and M. Morrison (eds), *The Supply Story*, London: Falmer Press.

Morrison, M. (1999) 'Temps in teaching: the role of private employment agencies in a changing labour market for teachers', *Journal of Educational Policy*, 14, 2: 167–84.

Mullett, M. (1994) 'Highlighting a grey area', in S. Galloway and M. Morrison (eds), *The Supply Story*, London: Falmer Press.

Chapter 7

So what can schools do?

Context: the art of the possible

Headteachers have to play 'the hand they are dealt' in terms of the overall education system they work in and the teachers that are either in their school or 'on the market'. But they do have a degree of control over some of the factors which have emerged as having an influence on the extent to which teachers enjoy their work. This chapter looks at recent findings about how schools can make their systems for recruiting good teachers as effective as possible and at some of the general aspects of the climate of school life which are likely to have a positive effect on teacher retention.

Our own research into what young people want from a career and their views about teachers and teaching shows that many of their concerns and reservations about a life in teaching echo the concerns of trainee teachers, NQTs and more experienced teachers. There would appear to be a strong element of social transmission here (see pages 16–17); a lot of people come into some contact with someone who is a teacher. The quotations from teachers in this chapter are drawn from interviews with 84 teachers (48 primary, 36 secondary).

No number of glossy magazines (see for instance, *Think Teaching!*), advertising campaigns, or courses to lure back members of the 'PIT' (Pool of inactive teachers), will keep people in teaching if it is not, in reality, an enjoyable and fulfilling job. In a well-intentioned attempt to attract third-year undergraduates into teaching, a group of 'teacher advocates' recently visited the university and presented a picture of a life in teaching as one of unremitting joy. Even apart from the fact that they were all employed in the independent sector, the portrayal of teaching as an unproblematic idyll aroused suspicion and antipathy rather than enthusiasm. It is not *just* a question of pay, or having enough money to become a home owner, it is about the quality of teachers' working lives. The way that teaching is presented has to have some basis in reality.

Our survey of sixth formers and third-year undergraduates across ten local education authorities and nine universities and a smaller scale survey of 194 of our own trainees showed that alongside pay, the principal factors which prevented teachers from enjoying their work were bureaucracy, workload and pupil behaviour. The findings are not markedly different to several other enquiries into teacher morale, recruitment and retention (Spear *et al.* 2000; Smithers and Robinson 2000; Guardian/ICM 2000; Kyriacou and Coulthard 2000; NUT 2000; NAHT 2000; Clough *et al.* 2002).

How are heads and senior colleagues to respond to such concerns, given that they are not free agents? They cannot wish Ofsted out of existence (and may not wish to), or opt out of SATS (whether or not they believe in them). They can't just ignore all DfES requests for information, or drop maths from the curriculum because they can't get any maths teachers. Heads and senior management teams have to work within the frameworks laid down, do their best with the location they are in and try to maintain a full cohort of well-motivated, high-calibre teachers in a situation where demand outstrips supply.

There are, however, some areas where there are parameters within which schools can operate and some things over which they have a degree of control. There is, for example, some evidence to suggest that some schools have reacted much more radically than others in the extent to which their procedures for advertising and interviewing posts have adapted to changing circumstances.

There is also the question of to what degree they enthusiastically embrace all government initiatives, push the take up of optional and world-class tests, interpret assessment and target-setting responsibilities, and 'mirror' DfES mentalities within their own schools.

To what extent can they respond to recent research findings (and their own knowledge) about what makes teachers enjoy their work and stick with teaching in spite of the negative aspects of their work? One of the sad ironies of our research is that teaching clearly has the potential to be a particularly rewarding and fulfilling occupation, and in many cases it fulfils that potential. As things stand, however, there are also many cases where it is very difficult for teachers to enjoy teaching. Many of our respondents stated that they enjoyed 'the actual teaching', but were disenchanted, considering getting out, or had already done so. One respondent remarked that teachers were 'not paid enough to put up with the crap'. To what extent is 'the crap' an inescapable part of teachers' lives? To what extent is it possible to get rid of, or at least minimise, the influence of things that stand in the way of teachers being able to enjoy their work?

In a system where accountability structures are centrally defined and where pay and conditions are determined by national agreements, there are areas where there are limits to what that schools can do to 'make a difference' in terms of some of the factors which influence the quality of teachers' working lives. Nor, in most cases, can they exert a substantial degree of control over which pupils will provide the raw materials that the teachers will be working with. In some areas however, heads and senior management teams can make a difference to the climate which teachers will be working in, in terms of both the working atmosphere in the classroom and the general atmosphere in the socially shared areas of the school, such as the staffroom and the office. They can also make a difference in the way that they put into effect the directives of policy makers, particularly in areas such as assessment and reporting arrangements and target setting.

Three overarching questions which heads might ask are:

1   How effective are our arrangements for recruiting new teachers?
2   To what extent can teachers enjoy their teaching in this school?
3   To what extent is this school an enjoyable place to work?

1 How have schools responded to the recent problems of teacher supply? How effective are arrangements for recruiting new teachers?

As outlined in Chapter 3, one of the most effective steps a school can take to attract teachers coming into the profession is to establish close links with partnership providers and develop a high-quality programme of in-school training and support for teacher trainees so that the attractiveness of the school will percolate the partnership 'grapevine'. There is also, however, the question of arrangements for the advertising of posts and interviewing of candidates.

Schools differ in the speed with which they process a vacancy, in terms of the length of time between the vacancy occurring and the date of the interview. Even in a medium-sized partnership like ours (with approximately 400 trainees per year), a few days can make a big difference in terms of how many of the highest calibre trainees are not fixed up with a post in many secondary subjects. In the words of Cathryn Stead, a member of Education Bradford's recruitment team,

> A lot of heads have been here a long time; the first time they recruited staff it was easy, but it's a different ball game now. For some it's quite a culture shock – heads used to advertise and wait for people to apply, but you've got to go out and grab the people available.
>
> (*TES*, 5 July 2002)

Even when a post is being advertised in the *TES*, many schools now phone, fax or email us with details of the post as it becomes available. Most curriculum tutors now have an email list for all their trainees and so can pass on details of the post to all members of their teaching group within minutes of receiving the information. In one case, a school was able to contact a curriculum tutor on a Bank Holiday Sunday, and interview three candidates for a post on Bank Holiday Monday.

Schools also vary in the extent to which they make use of electronic communication in their applications process. For most PGCE trainees, email is the instinctive, time-effective form of communication. Phoning schools can be a time-consuming process, as can posting applications. A recent *TES* survey found that under half the sample schools in the survey gave details of an email contact, and less than 10 per cent specifically welcomed email contact (*TES*, 9 May 2003).

The survey also found that few schools were using the potential of the internet to get information out to applicants quickly, or to use their website to best effect in terms of providing appropriate information for potential applicants. Only two of the 50 schools surveyed had job information on the site, and no schools gave detailed information about professional development opportunities for staff, staffroom facilities or other details which might be of interest to applicants – extracts from Ofsted reports, SATS scores, extra-curricular strengths.

It is difficult to overstate the part that the internet plays in trainee teachers' lives. Whereas three years ago, the instinctive first move of a trainee might be to go to the Ofsted website to look at the school's most recent Ofsted report, the most instinctive first step now is to look at the school's website, to get a more visually rich picture of what the school is like. The school's website is now an important part of how it presents itself to potential applicants for posts. Even where the generic school site has an impressive 'front-end', there are big variations in the extent to which departmental sections are developed, and this is a natural port of call for secondary trainees.

Developments in communications technology have also made it easier for schools to gain more depth of information on teachers applying from other countries. The 'Talking CV' service (www.mercershawmatthews. co.uk) makes it possible for schools to access five-minute video presentations by teachers who live abroad, by internet connection or by means of a CD posted to the school. It might not be as satisfactory as a full personal interview, but users found it more helpful than having to simply rely on a phone call and also commended the fact that the process could be conducted at a time convenient to the head or deputy, rather than having to be fitted around the school day (*TES*, 11 April 2003).

Information packs sent out by post were also found to vary in usefulness and the impression they gave of the school. One school mentioned that it had just been inspected and would be an Ofsted-free zone for the next four years, some were felt to have made good use of pupils' work in presenting an attractive image of the school, other information packs were described as 'dry as dust'. With some schools, there was little obvious 'differentiation' in terms of 'audience' and applicants were given information which was felt to be more appropriate for parents rather than potential members of staff, with details about school uniform, policy on 'nits', the agenda of the next parents' AGM and the date of the next school sports day. The survey concluded that:

> What schools did send to applicants was as diverse as the schools sending it. There were some common factors – schools assume, probably correctly, that the more senior the post, the more information is required. But if filling teaching posts with the right people is crucial, it is strange that so little of the information sent out is directed at the teacher.
>
> (*TES*, 9 May 2003)

In terms of our own feedback from trainees, a common complaint was the very tight timescale between advertisement of the post and closing date. Many trainees acknowledge that there are jobs that they would have been interested in, but that the deadline fell at a time when lesson preparation and marking demands made it difficult to find time to complete and post an application.

Trainees seemed to have no objection to the increasingly common practice of being asked to teach part of a lesson as part of the interview process and welcomed being given the chance to talk to pupils, or be shown round the school by pupils. Other facets of the interview process which evinced positive comments included being able to spend some time in the staffroom and the feeling that they had been shown 'the whole school', rather than selected highlights.

Several trainees expressed a preference for an informal style of interview, where they were invited in to have a talk to the head and head of department as an individual, but expressed reservations about this format where they were not given a clear indication of the status of the meeting and whether there were other applicants waiting to have a similar talk. A few trainees were put off by what they saw as a slightly aggressive or challenging mode of interviewing. In some secondary subjects, trainees have obviously come to see the interview as a two-way process. In the words of Catherine Parker, 'Today's candidates know that the market favours them, and they're going to ask what the school is prepared to offer them' (TES, 5 July 2002).

Although partnership providers are the largest and most obvious source of potential recruits, recent difficulties have led to a more eclectic approach to finding new teachers. One of the most obvious is the Graduate Teacher Programme (GTP). Although reports suggest that the quality of 'on the job' training is variable (Foster 2001; Ofsted 2002a), they also found that many schools provided high-quality training for GTP trainees and that the retention rates for GTP trainees compared favourably with that for PGCE trainees (Foster 2002). As suggested in Chapter 3, it seems likely that schools that have invested in providing a 'Rolls Royce' programme for trainees are likely to reap a better reward for their investment than schools that have simply used GTP to cover crises in particular staffing areas. The TTA is currently undertaking research and development work to improve the quality and consistency of GTP programmes (www.tta.gov.uk/itt/ebr/gtpreform/working. htm). As with conventional or traditional routes into teaching, the quality of selection and interviewing processes is crucial to the success of GTP. Getting the right raw material onto the course (or into the school) in the first place is at least half of the battle. Every second spent in careful exploration of both the capability and the personality of the applicant is time well invested. Our experience suggests that the area of 'Professional Values and Practice' – much more high profile in the recently revised standards for Qualified Teacher Status (QTS) (DfES/ TTA 2002) – is particularly important in this respect – will they 'fit in' with colleagues, will they be good to work with, and perhaps above all, will they be 'good learners'?

Another way of broadening avenues for recruitment, in tandem with the GTP, is for schools to be more proactive in exploring personal contacts. Whereas in the first instance, schools responded to enquiries and explored possibilities for classroom assistants, technicians and other ancillary staff, some schools have actively encouraged members of staff to be proactive in exploring possible contacts who might be suitable for the GTP. One school now has 15 per cent of its staff complement filled by former pupils, after systematically 'tracking down' and contacting former students and those of other local schools who had gone to university. Brenda Watson, the headteacher, claimed that the scheme had been particularly effective, partly because schools already had 'good intelligence' on the students' personal and academic qualities and also the pupils were familiar with the culture of the school in the area (*TES*, 21 December 2001).

Schools vary on the extent to which they are proactive in recruiting teachers from overseas, with some heads advocating trips abroad to conduct interviews with interested teachers (see, for example, *TES*, 27 July 2001), and others relying on a combination of agencies and the telephone. Although there are dangers that they won't arrive, won't stay or will find the British school systems and cultures difficult to adjust to, drawing on the pool of teachers worldwide clearly adds to school options in difficult subject areas and many schools have found outstanding teachers who have given years of valuable service. The degree to which schools can provide a reasonably relaxed and controlled working atmosphere in classrooms appears to be a crucial factor in determining the durability of teachers from abroad, but this is also a factor for home-grown recruits (see pages 60–64).

Another area of contention in teacher recruitment is the extent to which it can be satisfactory for teachers to teach 'out of field'. There is a degree of irony in the prevalence of this practice, given the very high emphasis on 'subject knowledge' in the standards laid down for the training of teachers (DfEE 1998; DfES/TTA 2002). There are two separate questions arising from this practice: one is whether pupils' progress is being jeopardised by the limited subject expertise of the teacher, the other is whether it is possible for teachers who are teaching a subject for which they were not trained to enjoy their teaching to the extent that they will stay in teaching.

The answer to the first question is that it depends of the context and that it is a matter of degree. Headteachers have to find the least-bad solution possible where there are shortage areas. Teaching out of field may be more manageable in some subjects rather than others. Many history and geography trainees teach other humanities subjects as part of their training and may also have taught English or modern foreign languages, according to their A-level subjects, but they are less likely to

be able to survive as teachers of maths. Another factor here is the exceptionally high calibre of PGCE trainees in some subjects, in areas where
there is not a teacher shortage. Many of our secondary history trainees
are keen to stay in the area after their training, but there are rarely as
many history posts in Norfolk and Suffolk as trainees seeking permanent
posts there. Many of them are very highly qualified in terms of degree
classification and A-level points score, and have proved to be outstanding
trainees on both their school placements. Where they have had to take
posts teaching English, geography, RE, sociology or 'filling in' generally,
as a sort of 'in-house' supply teacher, the feedback from heads has been
very positive. Many of them had progressed to middle management
posts outside their subject specialism, either as special needs or ICT
co-ordinators, or as year tutors in the school's pastoral team. A key factor
appears to be strength in terms of their overall professional attitude and
approach, and in particular, strength in area 1.7 of the Standards for QTS
– perhaps the most important of all the strands of the Standards in terms
of considering whether or not to take on a teacher or a GTP trainee:

> They are able to improve their own teaching, by evaluating it,
> learning from the effective practice of others and from evidence.
> They are motivated and able to take increasing responsibility for their
> own professional development.
>
> (DfES/TTA, 2002: 6)

In response to the second question about teaching 'out of field', we were
able to talk to six former trainees who had chosen to teach outside the
subject for which they were trained. All six appeared to be prospering
in their careers and were well thought of by their schools. Although
most of them expressed a degree of wistfulness about not being able
to teach their preferred subject, they all felt they had made the right
choice.

Five of them had taken a post in one of the schools where they had
undertaken their PGCE placement, and a key factor in their decision
was their enjoyment of the climate of the school in general – they had
enjoyed their time at the school, got on well with colleagues and found
it possible to enjoy their teaching because of the reasonable levels of
classroom behaviour which were prevalent at the schools they were
working in. One had chosen to move out of a school where he had
been teaching his own subject because of the levels of pupil behaviour and
had 'rediscovered' the enjoyment of teaching by becoming an English
teacher in a school where pupil behaviour was less problematic.

Several of the trainees in our survey of what they felt they would be doing in five years' time (see pages 80–2) expressed the aspiration to be working in teaching part time, and this mirrors recent reports in the educational press about the desirability of more flexible working patterns for teachers of all ages (see, for example, *TES* 21 September 2001, 3 May 2002, 28 February 2003, 4 April 2003). Although part-time teachers obviously create timetabling problems (or nightmares?) for school managers, Alan Smithers (2003), director for the Centre for Education and Employment at Liverpool University, suggests that it may be a *faute de mieux* solution, especially where schools may gain a good reputation for flexibility of working patterns:

> It may be good for schools as teachers who are parents would stay in the profession rather than leave, as quite a few do now. . . . There are also quite a number of teachers leaving because of heavy workload who intend to become supply teachers. They feel that supply work lets them focus on teaching and do less of the other activities teachers have to engage in. Maybe schools will create flexible hours for such teachers as a way of retaining staff.

As well as optimising the chances of luring teachers out of the 'PIT' (Penlington, 2002), this may also be a way of retaining effective and highly experienced older teachers who still enjoy teaching but do not enjoy the full workload that current working arrangements entail. A Scottish scheme which allows older teachers to work part time without jeopardising their pension arrangements has proved highly successful in retaining experienced staff, 'but ministers have no plans to introduce the incentive in England and Wales' (*TES*, 3 May 2002).

2 Attracting and keeping good teachers: to what extent can teachers enjoy their teaching in the school?

'Being able to teach'

Making sure that the school has the best possible arrangements and systems for recruiting new teachers and making the most of all possible contacts is one element of a successful strategy for attracting high-calibre teachers to the school, but it is quite distinct from the question of the extent to which teachers will find it possible to enjoy their teaching once they have joined the school. Much of the evidence about 'why teachers teach' points to the intrinsic satisfaction of teaching as a worth-while and enjoyable activity – given certain conditions. 'Being able to teach' emerged as an important consideration for many of the trainees and teachers we interviewed. The following extracts are from interviews with experienced senior teachers who had chosen to stay at the school they were working at in spite of opportunities to move on:

> 'I've stayed here because it's a school where you can enjoy most of your teaching . . . which is what you spend most of your life doing . . . that's what has kept me here, even though there is no A-level work in the school.' (Head of Department)

> 'One of the biggest things is the subject teaching – being able to go in and enjoy your subject teaching.' (Head of Sixth Form)

> 'Other people arrive here and think it's not too bad . . . they hear horror stories from other schools about disruption and feel that at least here it's OK. . . . It's somewhere you can stay and improve your teaching. They hear anecdotes and feedback from colleagues who have moved on and who have been unhappy with their move. There's a sort of comfort zone here. We don't do laptops for new staff, although it's a nice gesture.' (Assistant Head)

Given the overwhelmingly strong feedback from the survey of our trainee teachers (see Chapter 4) that the biggest source of (potential) job satisfaction was 'seeing pupils make progress', this raises the question of the extent to which the working arrangements in classrooms in the school are conducive to allowing pupils to make progress. The other high-frequency responses were 'working with children', 'pupils' response to learning' and 'good climate/atmosphere' in the classroom. But what if the working atmosphere in the classroom is not good, what if the pupils' responses to learning are hostile and negative, and working with children in classrooms is a difficult and draining experience?

Both the responses of our trainees and our interviews with practising teachers indicated that the working atmosphere in the classroom was an important part of their quality of life as a teacher. Many responses indicated that disruptive behaviour by pupils, the feeling that the learning of some pupils was being hampered by the poor behaviour of others, and the difficulties involved in getting a calm, purposeful and co-operative learning environment in classrooms were a major impediment to being able to enjoy the job.

Schools obviously vary enormously in the extent to which exemplary working environments are prevalent in classrooms and the percentage of classes where teachers or trainee teachers are in relaxed and assured control of the pupils they teach, not least because of the nature of the pupils in those classrooms.

The degree to which there are 'deficits' in the working atmosphere in classrooms is a contested area. According to the 2001 report of the Chief Inspector for Schools, behaviour was found to be generally good in over 90 per cent of schools in England and Wales. A subsequent report suggested that behaviour was a problem at one in 12 secondary schools, and one in 50 primary schools (Ofsted 2002b, 2003).

Other surveys suggest that poor pupil behaviour and deficits in the working atmosphere may be more prevalent than the Ofsted figures suggest (Moser 1994; Barber 1994, 1996). Some of our own research suggests that deficits in the working atmosphere in classrooms are not confined to inner-city schools (Haydn 2001), and in the survey of our own trainees (see Chapter 4), 87 of the 194 trainees felt that poor pupil behaviour was a factor that made it difficult for teachers to enjoy their work. Several indicated that standards of behaviour in classrooms was one of the factors that would influence their decisions on job applications.

Beginning teachers may obviously have a jaundiced perspective on pupil behaviour, but interviews with NQTs and more experienced teachers suggested that the problem of poor pupil behaviour was not limited to trainee teachers. Several teachers cited pupil behaviour as the main factor that prevented them from enjoying their work. The following extracts are all from teachers who are acknowledged (by their heads and colleagues) to be successful and experienced classroom practitioners and who have accomplished skills in classroom management. They work in schools which are oversubscribed and which are not considered to be 'at the sharp end'.

> 'I used to really enjoy the job, but haven't done so for the past few years . . . Biggest single thing is the behaviour of the kids . . . very draining, makes it difficult to actually enjoy teaching. I've got one Year 7 class who are a delight to teach, they're lovely, but it reminds me that nearly all the classes used to be like that.'

> 'You get worn down by the constant battle just to get pupils to do as they are told . . . it's a real effort just to enforce things that are supposed to be basic school rules.'

'At the end of the day, we've got kids here who are disruptive who never would have been disruptive but for the contact with these (disruptive pupils transferred from other schools) pupils. It's just anything to keep them off the streets . . . The impact he's had on other kids is phenomenal . . . within 10 seconds of going into X's classroom he'd thrown a chair at someone and kicked a cupboard in. This pupil hasn't benefited in any way, but there are kids that he has influenced . . . when they start to see chairs thrown around, they think that it is within bounds.'

Several surveys have indicated that pupil behaviour and the difficulties of establishing an enjoyable and controlled learning environment in the classroom are major factors in teacher retention (Spear *et al.* 2000; Smithers and Robinson 2000; Hutchings *et al.* 2002).

According to Alan Smithers, the principal reason for problems with teacher retention is bad behaviour by pupils:

There are changing attitudes in society and teachers are at the sharp end of it. They find that it is a continuous struggle to get children to listen and learn. Children are constantly challenging them and it is a battle to get them to do anything.
(quoted in *Guardian Education*, 4 September 2001)

Certainly, our own survey of sixth formers and third-year undergraduates found that perceptions of teaching were influenced by negative views about pupil behaviour, with a substantial majority agreeing with the statements that 'teachers must deal with violence' and that 'teachers deal with children who are difficult to control'.

The central importance of 'being able to teach' is illustrated by responses from teachers at Robert Clack School, Dagenham, where very high levels of support for teachers in establishing 'the right to learn' from the head, governors and the LEA resulted in major improvements in pupil behaviour, exam results and teacher morale. Teacher supply and retention is no longer an issue at the school and it attracts large numbers of applicants for most posts advertised.

'The triumph of the last two years is that now everyone can teach – you just go in there and teach.'

'The system is now tough on disruptive pupils – it has helped us to get stronger in the classroom.'

'Nothing but 100 per cent support – we're all in it together, we've all looked into the abyss.'

'Teachers know that as long as they behave professionally, they can stand up and the teacher will win.'

'He takes on pupils and parents where necessary, the sense of will gets through to pupils, you can get down to worthwhile teaching.'

'I never think about discipline any more, it's just about planning your lessons. It doesn't matter what time of week it is, I can do anything with them.'

'To come to this school, you have to abide by the rules.'

'Professional satisfaction – you're not wasting your time controlling kids, you can help kids to learn.'

'We've got on top of the problem of two or three kids spoiling the learning for others – that's now very rare.'

Heads and senior management teams might consider what percentage of classes are under the relaxed and assured control of teachers, to the extent that teachers could reasonably be expected to be able to enjoy their teaching. A 10-point scale which we have used with trainee teachers to get them to think about the working atmosphere in the classroom found that, for trainees, it is quite common for the 'level' to fall to an extent where it is not possible for them to enjoy the activity of teaching (Haydn 2002). In many schools, this may also be the case for qualified teachers. If the working atmosphere in the classroom falls below, say, level 6 on the scale, it is difficult to see how teaching can be an enjoyable activity. It could be argued that as soon as it falls below level 9, the extent to which teachers can enjoy their teaching is reduced. (The scale is reproduced in Appendix 2.)

Support

The main factor that will determine the standards of classroom behaviour and the working atmosphere in classrooms is the nature of the school's intake of pupils, although the quality of classroom teaching, and the teaching and behaviour management skills of individual teachers are clearly also important.

But there is also a 'school effect' which goes beyond the nature of the pupils which schools receive and the skills of individual teachers. Whole school policies can make a difference in this area, through the effectiveness of behaviour management systems, the extent to which schools can get colleagues to work collaboratively, and the degree of support which the head, senior colleagues and governors give to supporting the rights of pupils to learn and the rights of teachers to be able to teach in reasonable conditions. In many schools, there is a difficult tension between educational inclusion and not allowing pupils with problems to spoil the learning and life chances of other pupils. How schools handle these issues and tensions can have an effect on the extent to which teachers are able to enjoy their teaching.

This was reflected in our survey of the factors influencing trainees' decisions about which teaching posts to apply for and which factors persuaded them to accept a post, with 21 out of 59 trainees mentioning 'good support' or 'impressed with school discipline policy' as a factor influencing their decisions. In the larger survey of trainees, 35 of the 194 responses mentioned better support in dealing with disruptive pupils as one of the factors which would help to improve the quality of teachers' working lives. Several trainees indicated that they had preferred working in schools in challenging circumstances where there were clearly defined and effective systems for dealing with pupil behaviour to working in less difficult schools which had a more *laisser faire* approach.

Feedback from experienced teaches also suggests that one of the main factors which teachers are looking for in a head and in senior teachers is strong support in dealing with difficult and disruptive pupils. It would appear that there may be differing degrees in the extent to which schools offer this to teachers. There is obviously the danger that teachers may attempt to displace responsibility upwards and be seduced by the image of the heroic head who will solve all their problems and cope for all their inadequacies, but heads and senior teachers might ask themselves where the school stands in the 'support' continuum:

> 'In some ways, staff want the impossible . . . what they want more than anything from the head is that he is "the beast in the cupboard" . . . that when they say to pupils that something will go to the head, that they will be genuinely scared . . . This is one of the biggest things in the eyes of many teachers . . . that the head and senior

teachers will support them in getting good pupil behaviour so that they can enjoy their teaching.'

'You just get the feeling that he would be able to put the fear of God into them, but also, that he would be able to inspire them as well. He could operate at street level . . . sorting things out with parents, sorting out feuds on the estate . . . not afraid to take people on . . . a sense of will.'

'What staff love here about the assertive discipline policy is the "severe" clause – a senior member of staff hauls out a pupil who may be spoiling the lesson and removes them. It's only for about half an hour but they feel there is at least an immediate short term response . . . assistance.'

'What your colleagues are like is more important than what the kids are like in terms of your day-to-day morale. You accept that you're going to have to struggle with classes but as long as it's not all you . . . as long as you do get support when you're struggling to get control of a class.'

'At first the staff really liked him because he is such a nice person, but now they are screaming for support . . . he's just as nice with the kids but incapable of sorting them out . . . the school is quickly going down the drain.'

'New head . . . no support over discipline . . . good on paperwork, facades.'

'It's the constant having to justify yourself that wears you down . . . on the whole our SMT do their best but to some extent their hands are tied . . . A thousand last chances . . . Weeks of notice before you can exclude a pupil, having to draft individual action plans . . . while kids are charging round, disrupting lessons, being unbearable . . . Staff get frustrated.'

'The head feels he's there to support the child, or to settle things between teacher and pupil. I think that sometimes people in senior management forget what it's like having to teach all day everyday and cope with all the things that crop up and get in the way of being able to get on with your teaching.'

'In a school like ours you get a lot of pressure on middle managers, there are lots of initiatives . . . but that can make life interesting and exciting, and classroom management is not a problem . . . As a head of department I might have to talk to two or three pupils in the course of the year.'

'The head is very proud of our low exclusions rate . . . but the pressure falls on others . . . there are people in tears, at the end of their tether.'

Perhaps the most vituperative comments were reserved for heads who did not set a good example themselves in addressing serious incidents. The following vignette was written by a teacher who worked at a school which was in special measures for several years:

'You look down the corridor and notice what can only be described as chaos. Shouting, swearing – an aggressive bustle of pupils. It looks slightly dangerous, unruly and entirely inappropriate. It strikes you that you must do something, arrest the disturbance with a word, a command, an admonishment. You are about to speak, but then you notice . . . two figures beside the mob. One a senior manager, saying nothing. Two, a senior manager, turning a blind eye. As you make your way from classroom to staffroom, you meet with two pupils trying to leave 'the wrong way', contrary to the new one way system you're not entirely convinced about yourself. Still – follow the school line. You ask the lads reasonably, politely to turn back. They ignore you. You try again – less calm. They challenge you. Observers gather. As you address one boy, the other tries to walk through you. He walks into your arm. He tells you that you've hit him – you ought to let him through just to be on the safe side. And it occurs to you, as quickly as you are certain that you have done nothing amiss, that the support from above might not be there. That the rules, ultimately, mean nothing because nothing will be done. And you sense all along that this is what the pupils know – or they wouldn't be here, the gathering crowd, and this wouldn't have happened. And you wonder, why bother?'

Just as there is a 'grapevine' amongst trainee teachers about which schools are good to work in, there is (perhaps to a lesser degree) a jungle telegraph about the extent to which schools are 'under control' and the extent to which teachers will be supported in the area of behaviour management and in establishing 'the right to learn'. Teachers prefer to work in schools where they can enjoy their teaching and where they feel they will be well supported in dealing with the problems posed by difficult pupils. The comments of our trainees suggest that this is much more important to them than the level of academic standing of the school.

3 The quality of teachers' working lives outside the classroom: to what extent is the school enjoyable to work in?

Factors that can improve the quality of teachers' working lives

Many of the factors which have emerged as influential in recent surveys are 'soft' factors, such as 'friendly colleagues', 'pleasant surroundings', 'intellectual challenge', 'scope for creativity', 'freedom' and 'room for initiative', as against 'hard' factors such as 'status' and 'power' (Cockburn *et al.* 2000; Hutchings *et al.* 2002).

Many factors influence the extent to which teachers can enjoy their work outside the classroom. One major worry is the extent to which the schools' budget crisis, which pertains at the time of writing, may curtail schools' ability to respond to concerns which they know to be pertinent to teacher well-being. Some, but not all, of these concerns have financial implications, and at a time when many schools are struggling to avoid redundancies, there is a squeeze on non-staffing elements of school budgets. This is not to suggest that these areas are 'luxuries'.

One facet of this is the working environment and day-to-day working conditions of staff. In one school, a more collegiate and open approach to the stresses imposed by cover was felt to have improved staff morale:

> I think that there has been more sensitivity to the concerns and feelings of staff . . . A bit ago, there was an increase in staff absence and we talked about it as a staff and it came out that there was a bit of 'dread' and people feeling fed up about losing what few non-contact periods they had, so we made a decision to limit staff going out, for whatever reason, to no more than three a day, and this seems to have worked well.

In some cases, minor refurbishment of the staffroom was felt to have ~~med~~ the climate in which teachers worked, or sporting and social get togethers, chosen by staff rather than senior staff. In one case, just providing coffee in the staffroom was felt to have had a significant effect on the extent to which colleagues interacted with each other:

> We now have coffee and refreshments brought over to the staffroom at break so that staff no longer have to walk over to the canteen if they want a drink or something to eat. This has meant that a lot more staff come to the main staffroom at break time and talk to each other, instead of staying in prep rooms and dept offices. A few years ago it had got so that even at dinner times, colleagues hardly talked to each other, they just tried to catch up on their admin. Just things like putting table cloths on the tables at lunch – the food is OK, and most staff get together over lunch rather than just bringing in a sandwich and eating on their own as they were working.

Some schools have been more radical than others in being able to provide more planning time for teachers – either by making use of ICT to share the burdens of planning and preparation (*TES*, 14 June 2002, 18 April 2003), or by giving staff half a day a week in which they can do whatever they wish. Some schools have also been able to reduce the burden of cover by introducing a system of using a dedicated ICT suite to enable pupils to undertake self-directed learning when the regular teacher is absent, making substantial savings on supply teachers in the process.

Enhancing teachers' opportunities for continuing professional development (CPD) and giving them control over what form it should take are emerging as factors which have an impact on teacher retention. Several studies suggest that the quality of induction offered to new teachers is crucial to retention, particularly in the first few months (see, for example, Tickle 2000; Brown 2000). In a recent pilot scheme, NQT drop out rates in one London borough fell from 25 per cent to 5 per cent after the introduction of the Early Professional Development Scheme (*TES*, 21 March 2003) and also allowed schools to make substantial savings on advertising for recruitment. Even in the face of financial retrenchment to cope with budget shortfalls, some schools have resisted the pressure to cut back on the budget for staff development, supporting teachers to do MA work and freeing them to undertake research into their own practice. Although the idea of 'the reflective professional' has been under attack in an outcomes and competence driven era, there is evidence to suggest that giving time for teachers to undertake practitioner-based research, to work collaboratively with colleagues from other schools and to have greater control over their options for CPD are an aid to teacher retention (Hargreaves 1999; Brace 2002; Burns and Haydn 2002; *TES*, 21 March 2003). The DfES scheme for providing sabbaticals for teachers in challenging schools may be a helpful step forward, but much will depend on how munificently it is funded and how extensive opportunities will be (DfES 2001). The idea of teachers taking a pay cut of 20 per cent in order to fund such an opportunity themselves (*Guardian*, 26 September 2000) is likely to prove less enticing. One teacher spoke with some bitterness of the administrative burden of filling in forms for a frugal CPD budget:

> I spent hours filling in INSET forms; we didn't have to fill in any forms before and we got a lot more money for INSET a few years ago, the INSET budget is practically non-existent these days. If we had not been involved in teacher training it would have been non-existent. I can remember when I got a term off to do an MA and then a day a week for another term.

Management style

Hutchings *et al.* (2002) completed a study of teacher supply and retention in six London boroughs and identified issues related to school management as the most frequently given reason for leaving a job, cited by 45 per cent of leavers. Researchers from the same university conducted a survey of over 2,800 teachers across seven education authorities into what factors inclined them to stay in a school (Dalgety *et al.* 2003). With reference to school management, 87 per cent of respondents said that the most important quality for a manager was to be able to communicate effectively with their staff, followed by being supportive (70 per cent), approachable (65 per cent) and fair and consistent (59 per cent).

Our interviews with teachers focused principally on what factors inclined teachers to stay at a school rather than what had caused them to move on. There were several aspects of management style which appeared to have a significant influence.

The personality of the head and their concern for the well-being of teachers was a commonly cited factor, the head as 'reasonable human being', and this was seen as having a powerful influence on the overall 'climate' in the school. Four examples are given:

> 'They've got to shape a vision for the school, take it in a positive direction, but they've got to do it as supportive colleagues . . . first

amongst equals, not a hierarchy of authority . . . an emollient style of leadership, not being a manager, showing human qualities . . . you've got to have a range of social skills. Our head enjoyed a lot of respect because of his personality, the personality of the person at the top has an incredibly powerful influence on the atmosphere in the building. I know of one school where about a quarter of the staff are leaving, and the main reason is the management style of the head.' (Secondary Head of Department)

'I've stayed here because the heads and senior teachers have all been OK to work with and let you get on with the job. I did work for one head before I came here who was a really awful human being . . . getting at staff . . . out to get people. Certainly the new head is careful how he is perceived by staff . . . he's careful not to have favourites, keeps his distance from people generally, doesn't come in the staffroom apart from briefing, that is appreciated – or he knocks before he comes in – staff like that.' (Secondary Head of Department)

'The personality of the head is a key factor – are they approachable? They have to be OK as a person. Heads who will absorb the pressure on behalf of staff and not transfer it on to them. I have spoken to many primary teachers who really have been harangued and bullied. I just couldn't work in that environment . . . Support for teachers, for instance when dealing with aggressive parents . . . you know that an incident could happen to any teacher, it could be you next time. There was one school where we just didn't go when we were doing supply . . . we had heard the head screaming at a teacher who had had an incident with a pupil and a parent, you could hear her being screamed at from the other end of the building . . . There's a new breed of heads who "sweep in" with dynamic agendas for change, replacing more paternalistic older heads . . . Depends . . . have to set a good example themselves. They can be demanding in terms of their expectations of . . . how long must teachers stay after school hours . . . There's been a bit of a backlash against that . . . it can depend on how people are asked. Most people work very hard, you don't get many shirkers, and you know that the present head realises that . . . he says you can't stop after six o'clock, I'm closing the place up . . . he says you've got to get a perspective on the job, he's aware of the pressures on us.' (Experienced Primary School Teacher)

'Every now and then they would read page 247 of the management handbook which said that you had to be nice to your staff and they would lay on some sort of "do" without troubling to consult staff about what and when it should be . . . then not all of them would bother to turn up, or they would sit at their own table and talk amongst themselves. Sincerity was not a strong point.' (Secondary Head of Department)

Another facet of management style which featured in several interviews was the extent to which heads were sympathetically concerned with the development of teachers' careers, not just in terms of promotion, but also in terms of trying to ensure that teachers were enjoying their work, getting the opportunity to broaden their interests and enthusiasms, and sometimes looking sympathetically at requests for a career break, or the opportunity to undertake seconded work in teacher education at the university.

'The head is really good at wanting to do his best for his teachers, even when it might be difficult for the school to cover gaps . . . it's a sort of loyalty to colleagues.' (Secondary Head of Department)

'The opportunity for variety . . . new experiences . . . this has been one of the things that has been squeezed since the drive for standards . . . I've been at this school for a long time. It has helped that I got involved as co-ordinator for citizenship in the school, you can keep your enthusiasm. I'm looking forward to taking responsibility for the sixth form.' (Secondary Head of Department)

'Every year there's been something new for me . . . I've really enjoyed it. When there's nothing new it's probably time to move on. I do think on reflection that the head at my second school might have done more to encourage me . . . not just a question of points, but the feeling that you were being developed and nurtured . . . that that was part of the plan . . . that they were being a bit selfish in a way and not looking ahead. At this school I've been given something new to do every year . . . they're looking to develop me and the head has very much an open-door policy and is fantastic . . . there's a personal touch which makes you feel wanted and needed. You've got to be able to get up on a Monday morning and look forward to going in to work.' (Maths Teacher, now Head of Department)

'We have people here who have been here a long time, who aren't going anywhere and who still have ten years to go . . . We have unpaid assistant year heads, but they have been doing the job for some years – we could rotate things so that more staff are gaining pastoral experience . . . I just think that it would stop teachers going stale.' (Assistant Head)

Another strand to emerge from the interviews was the degree to which staff perceived the school to be directed by people within the school (whether leadership was distributed or not), or whether it felt as if the management of the school was primarily responding to the demands of outside agencies, such as Ofsted, the LEA, the DfES, strategies and initiatives. As Wilby (2001) points out, the moves towards the idea of the self-evaluating school may have 'conditioned' some schools into audit and outcomes systems which sit uneasily in school cultures, replicated DfES 'command and control' mentalities and reduced the intellectual autonomy of schools, 'Schools have internalised the control culture. They can create their own bureaucracy, test papers and assessment forms without any further intervention from external agencies.'

The School Teachers' Pay Review Body (2002) reported that 'detailed planning, administration, monitoring and recording have become a major contributor to the workload problem. This is now a serious threat to teacher morale and supply.' Although government policy and DfES administration are generally regarded as having had a negative influence on teacher morale, supply and workload, the PriceWaterhouseCoopers Report on the problems of teacher workload also identified some heads as prime contributors to increasing teachers' burdens (*TES*, 30 November 2001). Nigel De Gruchy, then leader of the NAS/UWT cited the example of a school where teachers were required to report on pupil progress every two weeks as an example of this:

> They have to describe what every child is going to achieve in another two weeks and then describe how they are going to move each child from where they are to where they want them to be. Overall, target setting is a good idea. But when it means teachers are having to study where children are every minute of every day, it's getting beyond a joke.
>
> (*Guardian*, 16 October 1999)

This may be an extreme example, but it raises the question about how happy teachers are about assessment and target-setting arrangements within particular schools.

One physics teacher we interviewed, who we knew to be very well thought of by the school's management team and colleagues and who had moved to a much lower salary in teaching after working in the computer industry, told us that 'If I hear the word target one more time, I'm worried I'm just going to thump someone.' He liked his colleagues, loved teaching and working with young people, but moved back into the computer industry because of 'all the bits that are nothing to do with teaching which dominate my life'.

'I love teaching but . . .' was a common strand in interviews. There was sometimes resentment where heads were seen to be more concerned with what Ofsted or the DfES wanted than what teachers within the school felt were important priorities.

> 'Many demands, initiative overload . . . the demand didn't come from staff, who were not consulted . . . the head wanted badges and logos to go on the school's letterhead . . . they saw it as an increase in the index of their success as a head . . . trophies . . . more bothered about virility than morale and fulfilment of staff . . . I just got cheesed off with assessment demands . . . Levels every four weeks.' (Secondary Head of Department)

> 'I left in the end and got out of teaching because of a combination of a negative Ofsted inspection, and a new head who was obsessed with Ofsted to an appalling degree.' (Primary Teacher)

> 'We have to give levels with percentage point levels twice a year. No one believes in this, it's just playing games.' (Secondary Teacher)

> 'Almost every initiative brings about an increase in bureaucracy, with a concomitant decrease in efficiency' (Secondary Head of Department)

> 'I love the teaching but I do feel worn down by some of the other stuff. Being here makes a difference . . . we're shielded from some of the worst excesses . . . The reporting system here is OK for instance, even though we do more than one report a year to parents, the process is efficient and streamlined . . . the format of reports provides good feedback to pupils but it only takes me about 20 minutes per teaching group. The head explains when things are necessary, and people on the whole accept this. We are aware that there are things which are not essential and that the head has made a judgement on . . . to dump

. . . so that we don't have to bother about them. It stops the admin burden from getting out of control. I have a friend who works at a school where it is not like this, and the staff have the full range of initiatives, audits and admin inflicted on them. It's not good for staff morale. It makes me realise how lucky I am to be here, in spite of the travel time.' (Secondary Teacher)

'He was quite quiet initially and I wasn't sure, but when it came to Ofsted, he was much more relaxed about the whole thing, and this had a big effect on staff, it wasn't such an ordeal and it seemed to go better – perhaps we were lucky in who we got, but his approach to the inspection made a big difference to staff morale.' (Secondary Head of Department)

In terms of moral responsibilities, Marie Stubbs, Head of St George's School, London identified her priorities as follows:

My first duty was always to my pupils, families, staff and governors. Everything else came second. If some new edict came from the DfES that I didn't feel was important, I'd bung it in the pending tray for three months and then bin it if I hadn't heard more about it.

(*Guardian Education*, 15 April 2003)

At a meeting of head teachers, Tim Brighouse urged heads to treat commands from government and their LEAs with 'a healthy degree of insubordination' and Maureen Burns, Director of the DfES innovation unit, commended a head who had given pupils an unauthorised extra day off so that the staff could have extra training (*TES*, 21 February 2003). Several of the teachers' comments indicated that they would prefer to work in a school that was being run by the management and teachers of the school rather than by the DfES or Ofsted.

This seems to be related in part to teachers' self image as professionals, exercising autonomy and judgement over their professional situation. Harry Brighouse, until recently Professor of Education at the Institute of Education, University of London, and David Hart, General Secretary of the NAHT, blame excessive *dirigisme* for the drift of state teachers to the private sector, rather than superior pay and conditions (*TES*, 10 May 2002, 26 April 2002), and there is little in our trainees' responses (see Chapter 4) to indicate that they have any ideological preference for the independent sector – if anything there is an affection for the idea of the comprehensive school. At a BERA colloquium on teacher recruitment and retention at the University of Leeds in September 2000, Hazel Hagger argued that in order to attract the highest calibre graduates into teaching more stress should be placed on the intellectual demands on teachers and that more focus should be attached to this aspect of teaching in publicity campaigns. In a sense, part of the attraction of teaching, and the reason that it does not lose its interest and challenge, is the difficulty and complexity of teaching. Alistair Ross (2001) exemplifies the dangers inherent in 'strategy' management of teaching in quoting the modern foreign language trainee who had just enjoyed chanting Jolly phonics with pupils, 'Am I doing this for the next 14 years? Do I want to do this for the next 14 years?'

The importance attached to 'soft' factors can be discerned in both the Hutchings *et al.* study of what teachers hoped to gain by a job out of teaching (see Figure 7.1) and our own survey of third-year undergraduates and sixth formers (Tables 7.1 and 7.2).

One other element of management style which emerged from trainee and teacher comments related to the overall climate or culture of the school. Hargreaves (1995) identified a typology of school cultures, ranging from 'Traditional' (high control, custodial, formal), 'Welfarist' (relaxed, caring, cosy), 'Hothouse' (claustrophobic, pressured, controlled) and 'Anomic' (insecure, alienated, isolated, 'at risk'). The vocabulary used by trainees in describing the factors which influenced their decisions in applying for and accepting posts suggested a preference for 'Welfarist' as opposed to 'Hothouse' school cultures, tending towards the use of

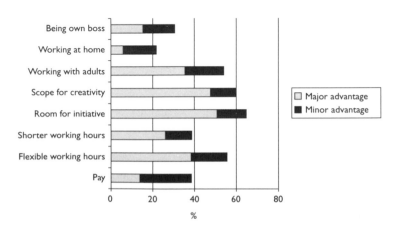

Figure 7.1 Advantages in new job over teaching (Hutchings *et al.* 2002)

Table 7.1 Factors most commonly cited as 'very important' in career choice by sixth formers (n = 1,675)

'Very important' factors	%
'Friendly colleagues'	72
'Job security'	69
'High potential earnings'	57
'Variety'	56
'Freedom'	49
'Scope to use initiative'	48
'Pleasant surroundings'	46

Table 7.2 Factors most commonly cited as 'very important' in career choice by third-year undergraduates (n= 346)

'Very important' factors	%
'Variety'	71
'Friendly colleagues'	66
'Scope to use initiative'	65
'Intellectual challenge'	60
'Job security'	47
'Scope for creativity'	45
'Pleasant surroundings'	45
'Freedom'	42

words such as 'relaxed', 'friendly' and 'laid back'. One school whose success indicators and credentials were quite impressive tended to be eschewed by trainees when vacancies occurred as it was felt to be 'overmanaged' or 'great for the pupils, not so good for the staff'.

The extent to which heads can get teachers to work together can also have a big influence on the extent to which the school is an enjoyable place to work. When asked what had persuaded him to stay at the same school, one head of department replied,

> The colleagues you work with, particularly at departmental level – to work within a good team with supportive colleagues – if adults are not working well together the job is much harder.

Another teacher who could easily have moved on to promotion elsewhere said,

> A few years ago, the staffroom wasn't that pleasant a place to come in . . . a few staff could be quite unpleasant, but now most of them have moved on, and it's OK now. I feel at times that I should be looking to move on, but in some ways I don't want to, I'm very happy working here, mainly because we all get on so well together and support each other.

Some schools seem to have been particularly successful in developing what Fullan (2000) terms 'lateral accountability', where there is a high degree of mutual support and trust between colleagues. Paul Grant, headteacher at Robert Clack School, Dagenham, which has seen rapid and sustained improvements in standards, pupil behaviour, teacher morale and teacher supply, questions the tabloid portrayal of 'welfarist' climates leading to a cosy conspiracy of teachers colluding in low standards and mediocre performance:

> It is not in their interest; a peer group of professional colleagues does not welcome into its ranks incompetent teachers. Colleagues have a very low tolerance level for such teachers, and on the very rare occasions when such teachers appear, they (the staff) demand that action is taken.
>
> (quoted in Haydn 2001: 426–7)

Grant argues that lateral accountability will only develop fully when there are high levels of trust between colleagues, and between teachers and school managers, and when all teachers feel fully valued and supported. A key feature of the success of Robert Clack was the very high level of support given to teachers by the head, the governors and the LEA. Grant identified the pastoral care and support of teachers as being the most urgent issue when he took over as head:

> Much of the publicity about education is predicated on the idea that there is a lot of inadequate performance – this is particularly damaging when a school has got a poor reputation – teachers have got to be looked after and supported, through actions, not just words . . . There were lots of good teachers who perhaps felt defeated and a bit downtrodden, who had lost confidence, who wanted to get out, or to retire . . . I had no agenda to divide and rule, or use successful units as a stick to beat the others with . . . If staff are giving many, many hours of time within and outside school working with pupils, and for pupils, fully committed to doing their best for the pupils in their care, they have got to feel valued and appreciated

. . . All coalitions and groups have got to work together; you've got to get everyone on board, everyone must feel that they have some value.

(ibid: 426–7)

What might policy makers do to help?

I Get rid of the 'floggings will continue until morale improves' approach

David Miliband's statement that the government would not do anything which damaged recruitment and retention (*TES*, 9 August 2002) will have evinced either a wry or a grim smile from many head-teachers, as will his letter to primary heads telling them to 'pull their socks up'.

There are some encouraging signs that the government is beginning to realise that teacher workload, bureaucracy, pupil behaviour and pupil disaffection are a problem, but there is still a reluctance to acknowledge fully the unintended effects of many government interventions over the last decade.

The distortion of school effectiveness and school improvement research to advocate the 'taking out' of failing heads and the use of successful schools as a stick to beat the others with has not been helpful to either school standards or teacher recruitment and retention. It has given policy makers a convenient tool to displace blame on to 'incompetent' teachers and 'weak' leadership as the *main* reason for low test scores and poor exam results in schools.[1] As Peter Mortimore (1999a) argued, the most that was ever claimed for 'school improvement' was that it might have a modest effect on school standards – at most 8–10 per cent.

> And so the Department for Education and Ofsted were committed to hunting down failing schools and attributing their failure entirely to the weakness of teachers and managers, ignoring the destructive impact of an intake which has become progressively more delinquent as the new poverty swept through the country . . . Whilst some schools can succeed against the odds, the possibility of them all doing so, year in year out, still appears remote, given that the long term patterning of educational inequality has been strikingly consistent throughout the history of public education in most countries . . . We

must beware of the dangers of basing a national strategy for change on the efforts of outstanding individuals working in exceptional circumstances.

(Mortimore 1999b)

Some DfES statements still echo Chris Woodhead's exhortation from 1996 to 'keep up the pressure' on teachers. One suggestion was that there should be 'spot check' inspections of schools (*TES*, 17 July 2001). What do we usually want to have spot checks on? Drunken drivers, people who steal things from work, people that we do not trust. What messages does this send to teachers? Teachers get slagged off enough in the papers, without the DfES joining in.

The past decade has seen a massive strengthening of systems to make teachers and schools accountable, but as well as having had some positive effects on the education system, it has had some negative ones as well. The apparatus of assessment and testing, audit and target setting, inspection and review, the moves towards direction by centrally imposed strategies, and the unremitting stream of initiatives from the centre have deterred substantial numbers of intelligent graduates and professionals from going into or staying in teaching. The DfES should at least consider the possibility that the pendulum has swung too far and that we are not at the optimum point on the continuum between accountability and professional responsibility.

2 Acknowledge teacher professionalism

McCulloch *et al.* (2000) point out the displacement in policy making circles of Keynesian ideals of public service by the tenets of 'new public management':

> This influential discourse tends to reject the notion of public sector workers as dedicated professionals applying their specialist knowledge to further the well-being of their clients. Instead, it depicts them as self-interested individuals, motivated by extrinsic rewards and in need of management and regulation.
>
> (pp. 104–5)

This might be entirely appropriate for 'fat cat' executives, but it is not an intelligent approach for graduates who have chosen to work in what is at present a difficult, unglamorous and not spectacularly well paid profession. There are not that many people desperate to become headteachers at the moment, without anyone exhorting governing bodies to 'take a few out'.

As Sennett (2000) argues, the government simply does not trust the public sector to regulate itself, with the result that 'it still has to grapple with the demoralising, soul-deadening bureaucracy which makes talented people think about doing something else or going elsewhere'.

The government's own Performance and Innovation Unit (2001), in a report that may not yet have reached the DfES argues that

> Excessive directive methods of government control that appear to treat front-line deliverers as unable to think for themselves, untrustworthy or incompetent, undermine the very motivation and adaptability on which real world success depends . . . Driving through school policies with an implicit assumption that the main players are the problem rather than the solution is usually a recipe for failure.[1]

The government needs to demonstrate trust in the professionalism of teachers; the most likely outcome of this is that standards will not go down and teacher recruitment and retention will improve. Nobody is trying to do it badly; and many teachers are working in conditions which are simply beyond the comprehension of civil servants. Perhaps, as Lord Puttnam suggests (2001), all civil servants at the DfES should do a stint in Bash Street, 'if for no other reason than to understand what it's like at the sharp end'. This is not a specious suggestion. Statistics giving the percentage of pupils on free school meals do not give a full picture of what it is like to work in a challenging school. A short (six months?) secondment to one of Britain's most difficult schools would give policy makers a more developed awareness of the grim reality of working in desperate circumstances, the complexity of factors influencing low attainment by pupils and imbue them with a more appropriate degree of humility.

3 Listen to what teachers and headteachers say and take their advice

If more than 90 per cent of teachers think that a particular initiative is a bad idea, then it is probably a bad idea, especially when research evidence supports that advice. This is not to advocate a return to 'the secret garden' of the curriculum, but to argue that serious thought needs to be given to the considered views of professionals. In a sense, teachers in the front line really do know what works best, what works and what does more harm than good. Cabinet Office ideas might be 'floated' before a panel of headteachers before they are taken further. Not all initiatives will be successful, and ones which are not should be abandoned. The online basic skills tests for QTS, which do so much to exasperate and dispirit the overwhelming majority of trainees, would be a good place to start, as a demonstration of intent.

4 Reduce prescription and bureaucracy

Our findings suggest that this is right at the top of the list of factors which alienate trainee teachers. Johnson and Hallgarten (2002) argue (along with many other researchers in this area) for a move away from the central imposition and rigorous policing of narrow targets which serve to demoralise the profession and deprive it of the qualified autonomy and creativity expected in the graduate labour market. They suggest a review of the whole target-setting process and urgent action to restore teacher autonomy, reduce workload and improve support over pupil behaviour.

Teachers do not go into the profession for money, for power, to compete for the biggest headships, or to win awards. They do it because it is an interesting, worthwhile and potentially enjoyable job, and they generally want to do the best for the pupils in their care. A large part of the fulfilment to be derived from teaching is knowing that you are doing it well and getting better at it. In the words of Penelope Lively, 'the point was not to make money, but to do something as well as it could possibly be done'.

'Why teachers teach' needs to be clearly understood by policy makers if this country is to attract the most committed, talented and intelligent graduates into the teaching profession, and keep them in it.

Note

1   I am grateful to Joe Hallgarten of IPPR for drawing this quotation to my attention.

References

Barber, M. (1994) Keele University Survey, quoted in the *Guardian*, 23 August.
Barber, M. (1996) *TES*, 5 April.
Brace, G. (2002) 'Training? They're biting our hands off for more', *TES*, 17 May.

Brown, K. (2000) Paper presented at BERA symposium on teacher recruitment and retention, University of Leeds, September.

Burns, B. and Haydn, T. (2002) 'Engaging teachers in research: inspiration versus the daily grind', *Pedagogy, Culture and Society*, 10, 2: 301–21.

Clough, J., Dalton, I. and Trafford, B. (2002) *What's It All About?*, London: DfEE.

Cockburn, A., Haydn, T. and Oliver, A. (2000) 'The psychology of career choice and young people's perceptions of teaching as a career', paper presented at British Psychological Society, Institute of Education, University of London, 19 December.

Dalgety, J., Hutchings, M. and Ross, A. (2003) 'Kind heads win loyalty of staff', *TES*, 4 April.

DfEE (1998) *Teaching: High Status, High Standards: Requirements for Courses of Initial Teacher Training*, London: DfEE.

DfES (2001) *A Sabbatical Scheme for Experienced Teachers in Challenging Schools*, London: DfES.

DfES/TTA (2002) *Qualifying to Teach: Professional Standards for Qualified Teacher Status in Initial Teacher Training*, London: DfES/TTA.

Foster, R. (2001) 'The graduate teacher route to QTS – motorway, by-way or by-pass', internal paper, Edge Hill College, fosterj@edgehill.ac.uk.

Foster, R. (2002) '"The carrot at the end of the tunnel": appointment and retention rates of teachers trained on the graduate teacher programme and a full time PGCE compared', paper presented at BERA Conference, Exeter, 13 September.

Fullan, M. (2000) 'Infrastructure is all', *TES*, 23 June.

Guardian/ICM (2000), *Guardian*, 7 March.

Hargreaves, D. (1995) School culture, school effectiveness and school improvement, School Effectiveness and School Improvement, 6, 1: 23–46.

Hargreaves, D. (1999) *Creative Professionalism*, London: Demos.

Haydn, T. (2001) 'From a very peculiar department to a very successful school: transference issues arising out of a study of an improving school', *School Leadership and Management*, 21, 4: 415–39.

Hutchings, M., Menter, I., Ross, A. and Thomson, D. (2002) 'Teacher supply and retention in London – key findings and implications from a study of six boroughs in 1998–9', in I. Menter, M. Hutchings and A. Ross (eds), *The Crisis in Teacher Supply*, Oakhill, UK: Trentham, 175–206.

Johnson, M. and Hallgarten, J. (eds) (2002) *From Victims of Change to Agents of Change*, London: IPPR.

Kyriacou, C. and Coulthard, M. (2000) 'Undergraduates' views of teaching as a career choice', *Journal of Education for Teaching*, 26, 2: 117–26.

Mortimore, P. (1999a) *Road to Improvement*, London: Cassell.

Mortimore, P. (1999b) 'Writing on the classroom wall was ignored', *Guardian*, 14 September.

Moser, C. (1994) *TES*, 9 September.

NAHT (2000) 'Parents that heads dread', *Guardian*, 7 April.

NUT (2000) Survey of Teacher Morale, quoted in 'Constant criticism upsets teachers', *Guardian*, 3 January.

Ofsted (2002a) *The Graduate Teacher Programme*, London: Ofsted.

Ofsted (2002b) *Annual Report of Her Majesty's Chief Inspector for Schools for the Year 2001*, London: Ofsted.

Ofsted (2003) *Annual Report of Her Majesty's Chief Inspector for Schools for the Year 2002*, London: Ofsted.

Penlington, G. (2002) 'Who returns to teaching? The profile and motivation of teacher returners', in M. Johnson and J. Hallgarten (eds), *From Victims of Change to Agents of Change*, London: IPPR: 41–64.

Performance and Innovation Unit (2001) *Better Policy Delivery and Design*, London: HMSO.

Puttnam, D. (2001) 'Whitehall should get classroom experience says Puttnam', *Guardian*, 16 March.

Ross, A. (2001) 'Issues in teachers supply and retention', paper given at the Future of the Teaching Profession Conference, University of North London, 27 April.

School Teachers' Pay Review Body (2002) *Report of the School Teachers Review Body on Teachers Pay*, London.

Sennett, R. (2000) 'The suffering professionals', *Guardian*, 18 October.

Smithers, A. and Robinson, P. (2000) *Attracting Teachers: Past Patterns, Present Policies, Future Prospects*, Liverpool: CEER/Carmichael.

Smithers, A. (2003) 'Part-timers time has come', *TES*, 28 February.

Spear, M., Gould, K. and Lee, B. (2000) *Who Would be a Teacher? A Review of Factors Motivating and Demotivating Prospective and Practising Teachers*, Slough: NFER.

Tickle, L. (2000) *Teacher induction: the way ahead*, Buckingham, Open University Press.

Wilby, P. (2001) 'Culture change puts enemy within schools', *TES*, 21 September.

Appendix 1

UNIVERSITY OF EAST ANGLIA SCHOOL OF EDUCATION AND PROFESSIONAL DEVELOPMENT

Careers questionnaire

Thank you for taking the time to read this. We are trying to find out how people decide on their careers and, in particular, what makes individuals opt for teaching or not as the case may be. It would be great if you could complete this short questionnaire to help us in our research. We can assure you that any information you provide will be treated in confidence and that no individual will be identifiable in the research report.

If you are at school please place your completed form in the large envelope and hand it in to your teacher. If you are at College/University please return your form in the attached envelope within 7 days.

Thank you

PLEASE USE BLOCK CAPITALS, BLACK OR BLUE INK
AND DO NOT FOLD THIS FORM – THIS IS
IMPORTANT FOR PROCESSING.

BACKGROUND INFORMATION

Please complete the following details about yourself by filling in appropriate boxes:

Q1   Sex   Male   ○   Female ○   Q2   Age   years

Q3   Ethnic Group

Bangladeshi   ○   Indian   ○

Black-African   ○   Pakistani   ○

Black-Caribbean   ○   White   ○

Chinese   ○

Other (please specify)

Q4   Do you consider yourself to have a disability?   Yes ○   No ○

(Optional) If you wish to please specify

Q5   Which School or University are you studying at?

School

College or
University

Q6a   If at School,

(a)   how many GCSE's (grades A-C) have you got?

(b)   what of the following do you hope to gain

1 A Level   ○   B Tec   ○

2 A Levels   ○   Further GCSEs   ○

3 or more A Levels ○   City & Guilds   ○

GNVQ's   ○   Other   ○

Q6b   If you are at College/University, what is your course and subject?

BA   ○   BSc ○   HND ○

Subject

Q7a   Have you decided which career you would like to follow?

No idea ○   Vague idea ○   Yes, probably ○   Yes, definitely ○

Q7b   If you can please say which career you would like to follow

FACTORS INFLUENCING CAREER CHOICE

Q8   The following list includes many factors that people think are important in a job. We want to know how important they are to you. Please fill in one box for each item on the list:

	Not at all important	Of some importance	Very important
1. Good starting salary	O	O	O
2. High potential earnings	O	O	O
3. Clearly defined career structure	O	O	O
4. Opportunity to help others	O	O	O
5. Holidays	O	O	O
6. High risk	O	O	O
7. Intellectual challenge	O	O	O
8. Job security	O	O	O
9. Predictability	O	O	O
10. Chance to be influential	O	O	O
11. Variety	O	O	O
12. Scope to use initiative	O	O	O
13. Working with adults	O	O	O
14. Working with children	O	O	O
15. Pleasant surroundings	O	O	O
16. Friendly colleagues	O	O	O
17. Freedom	O	O	O
18. Status	O	O	O
19. Scope for creativity	O	O	O
20. Power	O	O	O
21. Routine	O	O	O

Q9   Please list three of the above factors in their order of importance for you.

1. └──┴──┘

2. └──┴──┘

3. └──┴──┘

TEACHING AS A CAREER

Q10 Have you ever considered teaching as a career? Please fill in the circle which applies to you:

Yes, that is what I would like to do	O	please go to Q11
Yes, and it is still a possibility for me	O	please go to Q11
Yes, but have decided against it	O	please go to Q11
No	O	please go to Q12

Q11 If you have considered or are still considering teaching, what age group had you thought about teaching?

Primary	O
Secondary	O
Higher/Further	O
Not sure	O

Q12 What puts you off teaching as a career? Please fill in as many of the following list as are appropriate.

1. Controlling large groups	O	10. Long hours	O
2. Speaking to large groups	O	11. Paper work, administration	O
3. Teaching a subject to exam level	O	12. Pay	O
4. Perceived stress levels in the profession	O	13. School inspections	O
5. Teachers in the family	O	14. Working with children	O
6. Other people's attitudes to teachers	O	15. Not fitting in	O
7. Personal experiences at school	O	16. Lack of appropriate qualifications	O
8. Need to control difficult pupils	O	17. Not confident enough	O
9. Television and newspaper coverage	O		

Is there anything else which puts you off teaching?

_____

Q13 Please place in order of importance three of the above reasons for not wanting to teach:

1. ____

2. ____

3. ____

Q14 Would a £5,000 payment from the government influence your decision to choose teaching as a career?(This payment would be in addition to any student loans, grants etc and would be payable to all students studying for teaching qualifications)

Not at all O   A little   O   A lot   O

Q15 Are there any teachers in your family?   Yes O   No O

ATTITUDES TO SCHOOL AND TEACHING

Q16   Please write 5 words to describe your feelings about a primary school AND secondary
       school you attended as a pupil.

(a)   Primary School   (b)   Secondary School

1. |_____| 1. |_____|

2. |_____| 2. |_____|

3. |_____| 3. |_____|

4. |_____| 4. |_____|

5. |_____| 5. |_____|

Q17   Please consider the following statements and fill in the appropriate box to show how
       much you agree or disagree with them:

	Strongly agree	Agree	Disagree	Strongly disagree
Most teachers work very hard	○	○	○	○
Teaching is easy	○	○	○	○
Most teachers have time for hobbies	○	○	○	○
Teaching is enjoyable	○	○	○	○
Most teachers deserve their holidays	○	○	○	○
Teaching is for people who cannot think what else to do	○	○	○	○
You need to be clever to be a teacher	○	○	○	○
Teaching is a secure job	○	○	○	○
Teachers are poorly paid	○	○	○	○
Teachers deal with children who are difficult to control	○	○	○	○
Teachers have high status	○	○	○	○
Teachers must deal with violence	○	○	○	○
Teachers are bossy	○	○	○	○
Teachers are isolated	○	○	○	○
Teaching is about team work	○	○	○	○

Q18   If you are willing to take part in a short interview about career choices please fill
       in the following details here:

Name |_____|

Address |_____|
         |_____|

E mail |_____|

*Any information you provide is completely confidential. Please use the attached envelope to return your
questionnaire.* **THANK YOU**

Appendix 2

Level 10 You feel completely relaxed and comfortable; able to undertake any form of lesson activity without concern. 'Class control' not really an issue – teacher and pupils working together, enjoying the experiences involved.

Level 9 You feel completely in control of the class and can undertake any sort of classroom activity, but you need to exercise some control/authority at times to maintain a calm and purposeful working atmosphere. This can be done in a friendly and relaxed manner and is no more than a gentle reminder.

Level 8 You can establish and maintain a relaxed and co-operative working atmosphere and undertake any form of classroom activity, but this requires a considerable amount of thought and effort on your part at times. Some forms of lesson activity may be less calm and under control than others.

Level 7 You can undertake any form of lesson activity, but the class may well be rather 'bubbly' and rowdy; there may be minor instances of a few pupils messing around on the fringes of the lesson but they desist when required to do so. No one goes out of their way to annoy you or challenges your authority. When you address the class, they listen in silence, straightaway.

Level 6   You don't really look forward to teaching the class, it is often a major effort to establish and maintain a relaxed and calm atmosphere. Several pupils will not remain on task without persistent surveillance/ exhortation/ threats. At times you feel harassed, and at the end of the lesson you feel rather drained. There are times when you feel it is wisest not to attempt certain types of pupil activity, in order to try and keep things under control. It is sometimes difficult to get pupils to be quiet while you are talking, or stop them calling out, or talking to each other at will across the room *but* in spite of this, no one directly challenges your authority, and there is no refusal or major disruption.

Level 5   There are times in the lesson when you would feel awkward or embarrassed if the head/a governor/an inspector came into the room, because your control of the class is limited. The atmosphere is at times rather chaotic, with several pupils manifestly not listening to your instructions. Some of the pupils are in effect challenging your authority by their dilatory or desultory compliance with your instructions and requests. Lesson format is constrained by these factors; there are some sorts of lesson you would not attempt because you know they would be rowdy and chaotic, *but* in the last resort, there is no open refusal, no major atrocities, just a lack of purposefulness and calm. Pupils who wanted to work could get on with it, albeit in a rather noisy atmosphere.

Level 4   You have to accept that your control is limited. It takes time and effort to get the class to listen to your instructions. You try to get onto the worksheet/written part of the lesson fairly quickly in order to 'get their heads down'. Lesson preparation is influenced more by control and 'passing the time' factors than by educational ones. Pupils talk while you are talking, minor transgressions (no pen, no exercise book, distracting others by talking) go unpunished because too much is going on to pick everything up. You become reluctant to sort out the ringleaders as you feel this may well escalate problems. You try to 'keep the lid on things' and concentrate on those pupils who are trying to get on with their work.

Level 3   You dread the thought of the lesson. There will be major disruption; many pupils will pay little or no heed to your presence in the room. Even pupils who want to work will have difficulty doing so. Swearwords may go unchecked, pupils will walk round the room at will. You find yourself reluctant to deal with transgressions because you have lost confidence. When you write on the board, objects will be thrown around the room. You can't wait for the lesson to end and be out of the room.

Level 2   The pupils largely determine what will go on in the lesson. You take materials into the lesson as a manner of form, but once distributed that will be ignored, drawn on or made into paper aeroplanes. When you write on the board, objects will be thrown at you rather than round the room. You go into the room hoping that they will be in a good mood and will leave you alone and just chat to each other.

Level 1   Your entry into the classroom is greeted by jeers and abuse. There are so many transgressions of the rules and what constitutes reasonable behaviour that it is difficult to know where to start. You turn a blind eye to some atrocities because you feel that your intervention may well lead to confrontation, refusal or escalation of the problem. This is difficult because some pupils are deliberately committing atrocities under your nose, for amusement. You wish you had not gone into teaching.

The scale was devised to encourage trainee teachers to think about factors influencing the working atmosphere in the classroom, and the influence of the working atmosphere in classrooms on teaching and learning.

From Haydn, T. (2002) 'The working atmosphere in the classroom and the right to learn', *Education Today*, 52, 2: 3–10.

Index

This index is in word by word alphabetical order. References to tables and figures are given in bold print.